FABIAN CAPOMOLLA AND MAT PEM[...]

THE
LITTLE
VEGGIE
PATCH
CO.

How to grow food in small spaces

plum. Pan Macmillan Australia

To Beck, Jack and Olive, with love.

–Fabian

To my Nonna, my second mum;
and to my Nonno, my second dad I wish I'd known much longer.

–Mat

Introduction vii
Climatic zones of Australia xii

VEGGIE PATCH

FUNDAMENTALS

DESIGNING A VEGGIE PATCH 4
UNDERSTANDING YOUR SOIL 8
How to test the pH level of
  your soil 12
RAISED GARDEN BEDS 14
How to build a basic raised
  garden bed 16
NO-DIG (LAZY) GARDENING 19
How to layer a no-dig apple crate 21
THE IMPORTANCE OF WATER 24
How to install a drip
  irrigation system 27
SOWING YOUR SEEDS 31
How to propagate peas 34
SAVING YOUR SEEDS 37
How to save tomato seeds 40
EVERYONE SHOULD COMPOST 43
How to make a compost aerator 46
THE BENEFITS OF WORMS 49
How to make a worm farm 51
GROWING FRUIT TREES 54
How to plant a fruit tree 56

A–Z OF EDIBLE PLANTS

Apple 65
Artichoke (globe) 67
Asparagus 70
Beans 72
Beetroot 74
Bok choi/pak choi 76
Broad beans 83
Broccoli 85
Brussels sprouts 87
Cabbage 89
Capsicum 93
Carrot 95
Cauliflower 97
Celery 100
Chilli 107
Cucumber 109
Eggplant 111
Fennel 113
Garlic 115
Herbs 117
Leek 125
Lemon 129
Lettuce 131
Lime 135
Mushroom 137
Olive 141
Onion 143
Orange 145
Parsnip 152
Passionfruit 154
Peas 156
Potato 159
Pumpkin 161
Radish 164
Rocket 170
Silverbeet 172
Spinach 174
Spring onion 176
Squash 179
Strawberry 181
Swede 183
Sweetcorn 185
Tomato 193
Turnip 195
Zucchini 197

PESTS AND DISEASES

PESTS 205
DISEASES 215

WEEKEND ACTIVITIES

WHERE DOES OUR FOOD
COME FROM? 79
Growing beans in a bean can
USING RECYCLED MATERIALS
IN YOUR VEGGIE PATCH 103
Building a golf-club trellis
STOP LOSING YOUR TOOLS! 121
Painting your garden tools
SCARECROWS 149
Building a scarecrow
SPUD TOWERS 167
Building a spud tower
WATER 189
Water games

NONNA'S KITCHEN

Stuffed artichokes 69
Cabbage rolls 91
Chilli oil 108
Marinated olives 142
Sugo 194
Zucchini flower broken eggs 199

Acknowledgements 219
Index 220

INTRODUCTION

Some of our earliest memories are of spending time in our grandparents' backyards. We both grew up in Italian families, so pretty much every Sunday lunch we would sit down to a plate of pasta made with *sugo* from the previous summer's tomato crop, then finish it off with a rocket and fennel salad that was grown no more than 20 metres from the table. After lunch we took the obligatory garden tour to harvest whatever fruit was in season, Nonno leading the charge if he wasn't already asleep on the couch. Figs, blood plums, grapes and prickly pears were often on the menu, but if all else failed, a 'Femminello' lemon, picked straight from the tree, might be peeled with a trusty old pocket knife.

Like so many other migrants new to this country, our grandparents brought with them skills they had learnt from a life closely connected to the land — an informal education passed down from their parents and grandparents, and if they were lucky, great-grandparents too. These skills were a way of life, a life linked to the seasons, and it proved hard to leave behind. When you look carefully, the influence of the migrant population can be seen in many Australian suburbs, surviving in the shape of an old, knotted fruit tree on a corner of your property. But shrinking block sizes and the trend towards larger living spaces is quickly removing the evidence of such a heritage.

Detachment from the land seems uniquely a blight of the Western way of living. For thousands of years, our hunting and gathering predecessors cultivated the land, not only to provide food for their hungry stomachs but also to soothe their souls. No doubt this legacy has left this natural urge within all of us to grow our own produce and provide for our families, an urge that Western society tries hard to resist. Instead we subscribe to the mantra 'we want, and we want it now', creating an economy that provides us with everything, whenever we may want it. This overwhelming Supermarket Culture has homogenised food production to a point where we are largely detached from its origins, its seasonality and, most importantly, its taste. In turn, this has detached our generation, and that of our parents, from the food on our tables.

Satisfying that natural urge to grow and provide doesn't mean you need to dress up in animal hide, and you're even allowed to shower if you choose. Your starting point may be as small as a few pots of herbs on a balcony, or as large as your space and enthusiasm allows. And remember, your kitchen garden doesn't have to look like one you've seen in a fashionable landscape architecture book. We can attest that many migrant gardens aren't pretty, but they are productive. They all started with varying degrees of a few vital ingredients — light, water, growing medium and time.

The privilege of living in Australia means you don't have to grow food for survival, so instead focus your efforts on the pleasure of food. Grow food that you love. Grow things you will use in the kitchen but can't necessarily buy at the market. Grow food for whatever reasons motivate you.

The Little Veggie Patch Co exists because two people from similar backgrounds met and became motivated, and quite excited too, about their shared passion.

As it turned out, we had lived almost parallel lives, each joining our respective families in making *sugo* every autumn, making slightly different takes on very similar recipes for homemade sausage, regarding the smell of a tomato plant as one of our first memories and, generally, living a life that revolved around the kitchen. When we met for our very first catch-up in a café on Fitzroy's Brunswick Street in Melbourne, it quickly became clear we connected on the same fronts, right down to the thyme field mushrooms and polenta special and even ideas on how to maintain scruffy facial hair. A few meetings later, we had launched ourselves into the uncertainty of a niche business — 'helping people grow food for themselves'.

The first jobs involved setting up raised garden beds for our maiden clients. Our work in those early days followed a pattern of short, sharp bursts of activity punctuated by longer periods of inactivity, drinking strong black coffee and eating homemade muffins. We'd find ourselves locked in broad conversation, often with our clients too, about the work we were doing. Each time we met a new client and chatted with them, we found the common ground was food — the love of food, wanting to teach their kids where food comes from, the value of that knowledge, and in particular, the superior flavour of food that is grown chemical-free and eaten fresh off the tree or vine.

The more we sat down and the more coffee we drank, the more potential we could see in developing The Little Veggie Patch Co. Quickly our clients changed from solely space-endowed home owners to inner city renters, small businesses, kindergartens, schools and even corporations. Within a couple of years, the small movement of edible gardening had grown considerably, and regardless of the needs of each new client, there came the same *urge* to get started, somehow, some way.

As the type of clientele began to shift, the challenges of space and resources shifted and became amplified. No longer was it a matter of a raised garden bed here, a fruit tree there; increasingly we had to find ways of making the activity accessible and achievable to a greater range of people, regardless of whether they owned a suburban block or rented a balcony. In doing so it proved to them, and to ourselves, that growing food is not the time-consuming, frustrating, difficult beast it has been made out to be. And that is exactly what we hope this book will achieve too, especially when we can't be there.

The prospect of writing The Little Veggie Patch Co book developed each time someone visited our blog entry, 'How to build a raised garden bed'. It amazed us that such a simplistic step-by-step sequence of nailing timber together was what people wanted to see most. It highlighted that people wanted to know *how* to do it, rather than *why*. And that, quite simply, is the rationale behind our book.

Too many books on gardening become bogged down in the theory of growing food and ignore the practical side of doing so. *The Little Veggie Patch Co*, on the other hand, will show you *how* to go about it — logically, step by step. Easy-to-follow illustrations, replacing text-heavy theorising, will empower you to set up your kitchen garden properly, from building a raised garden bed and installing a drip irrigation system to composting and worm-farming, giving you the best chance of success. We have covered the food you *will* grow with an A to Z of edible plants and trees, and identified the pests and diseases you're likely to encounter along the way. There are even activities to help coax the kids into the garden and get their hands and clothes dirty all at once.

This book is for the idea-rich, time-poor person who dreams about harvesting the first tomato of summer and wants to get started *now* ... OK, *now*.

Fabian and Mat
September 2011

CLIMATIC ZONES OF AUSTRALIA

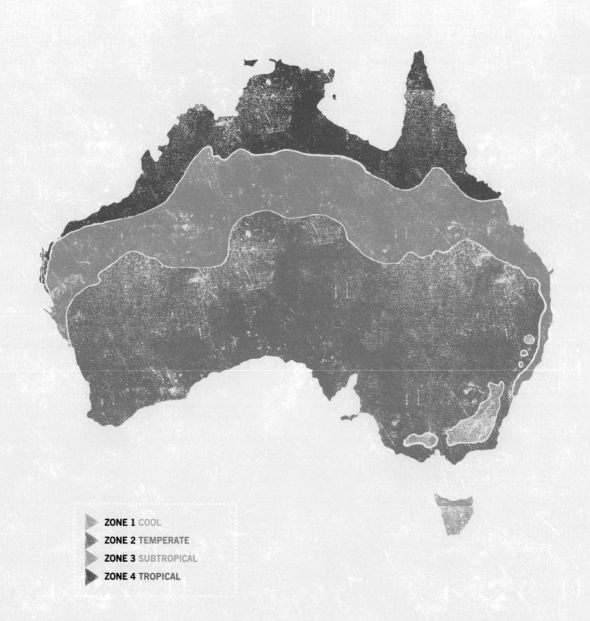

ZONE 1 COOL
ZONE 2 TEMPERATE
ZONE 3 SUBTROPICAL
ZONE 4 TROPICAL

WHERE AM I?

Contrary to what novice vegetable gardeners may believe, it is soil temperature, not air temperature, that dictates which vegetables may grow when, but of course using air temperature to determine what's going on down below is the best guide we have for planning and managing our veggie patches.

We Australians can consider ourselves privileged growers, ruled by a fairly relaxed and easy-going climate — our winter periods are relatively short and mild, without the severe frosts that disable other growers across the world, so we can grow and harvest all year round.

The first step in determining your potential vegetable-growing repertoire, and therefore using the information in this book, is to determine the climatic zone your veggie patch belongs to. Our zones are commonly broken into four groups:

> **1 Cool** Mild summer with cold winter and some frost. Includes high areas of the New South Wales Northern Tablelands, Southern Tablelands, Australian Capital Territory and Tasmania.

> **2 Temperate** Warm summer with cool winter. Includes inland Queensland, New South Wales Tablelands and coastal regions south of Sydney, and southern coastal Australia from Melbourne to Adelaide as well as southern coastal Western Australia, including Perth.

> **3 Subtropical** Warm, humid summer with mild, dry winter. Includes the eastern seaboard, from Sydney to Brisbane.

> **4 Tropical** Hot, humid summer with warm winter. Extends across the north of Australia, from Canarvon through Port Hedland and Broome in Western Australia to Darwin in the Northern Territory and Cairns and Townsville in Queensland.

Capital cities

Most Australians live in the state and territory capitals, so if that's you, simply check which climate zone your city belongs to:

> **1 Cool** Canberra, Hobart
> **2 Temperate** Melbourne, Adelaide, Perth
> **3 Subtropical** Brisbane, Sydney
> **4 Tropical** Darwin

Within the sketch:
DECKING

RAISED GARDEN
BED
3 SLEEPERS HIGH
WITH SEAT EDGE
- 2.9m x 1.2m

ROSE
BUSH
KEEP!

LEMON
TREE.

FENCE

SHADOW
CAST

GARDEN BED

AREA

HILLS
HOIST

DESIGNING
A VEGGIE
PATCH

The prospect of creating an edible garden can be so all-consuming, it's quite easy to get over-excited. Spurred on by the overwhelming urge to become self-sufficient, you find yourself staying up past midnight, a glass of red wine in one hand and a blunted pencil in the other, feverishly mapping the layout of your new veggie garden.

You are certain your family will share your enthusiasm and that trips to the supermarket will soon be a thing of the past. It all seems relatively straightforward. From what you can deduce, the hardest thing will be telling your partner their tool shed is now the chicken coop, and explaining to the kids that their cricket pitch will soon be an amazing new fruit orchard.

Just as you are about to put in your internet order for what is claimed to be an authentic Finnish Landrace goat, an overwhelming hot rush climbs up your spine to fill the last remotely sensible part of your brain. How the hell will we fit in the yabby pond?!

When designing your garden, the important thing is balance. You need to find a balance between your overwhelming enthusiasm, your needs and the means at your disposal. A well-designed garden functions by being practical, productive and aesthetically pleasing.

Location

Ideally, your veggie patch should be in a position that's accessible from the kitchen, so that venturing back and forth to collect your veggies doesn't become as tedious as a trip to the supermarket. There is little value in plonking the patch on the only unused spot of the garden — that spot is probably vacant because it is damp, shady and tucked out of the way. Leave this area free for little critters to use as their secret den, or let it fulfil another function, such as a water collection point for a rainwater tank. If you're constructing your veggie patch on a balcony or in a courtyard, think about how that space currently operates and what effect your new growing endeavours will have on it.

Another factor to consider is sunshine, although you shouldn't become obsessed with the idea that you need full sun to grow vegetables. Position your patch so that it faces north and catches the winter sun when it is lower on the horizon. While sunlight is a necessary element, root veggies and leafy greens need a minimum of only 2–4 hours of direct or filtered sunlight, fruiting veggies a minimum of 4–6 hours. If you have a choice between morning or afternoon sunlight, always go for the gentler morning variety.

If lack of sunlight is a problem, consider increasing the amount of light in your growing area by using mirrors, or painting the fence a brighter colour.

As a general rule, make sure that larger plants don't overshadow smaller ones, making them compete for sunlight. As such, plant smaller plants on the northern side of a patch and larger ones on the southern. If afternoon sun poses a problem in summer, you will need to consider providing shade for your veggie patch, by either constructing an artificial shade barrier or investing in a natural one, such as a fruit tree.

If your site is sloped, don't be deterred, as this will help the overall drainage of the area, but remember that your garden beds or containers will need to be level so that water is used evenly throughout the patch. If your patch is uneven, you may start noticing differences in the growth of your plants — those in the lower section will be mostly growing proficiently while the unfortunate plants in the higher section will be struggling and thirsty.

Good air circulation will reduce the susceptibility of your plants to fungal diseases, so try to stay away from cramped and damp positions. However, very open and exposed locations are most susceptible to wind and frost damage. Think of your car after an icy winter's night — the side parked nearest a structure or building always sports less frost than the exposed side. The same applies to your garden. So when planting out your patch, consider which varieties are frost-tolerant or -intolerant.

Size

Most of us are living in increasingly confined spaces, so gardening in small, challenging spaces has become the norm.

The smartest decision you can make is to start on a small scale and focus your attention on making your veggie patch as productive as possible. Don't launch yourself into subsidising your current food needs, let alone becoming self-sufficient. And, more importantly, grow things you absolutely love and will use in the kitchen.

Keep things manageable — you don't want to risk becoming overwhelmed by the size of your garden or the number of hours it consumes, and so end up neglecting it.

When considering the size of your veggie patch, ask yourself the following questions:

> How many veggies do you want to grow?

> How many veggies can you manage to grow?

A space that's a couple of square metres in area will allow you to plant a good variety of herbs and vegetables that you can add to at a later date.

For apartment dwellers or renters who don't want to overcapitalise, pots may be the best way to go. These are a perfectly good way to grow food, and are particularly suited for growing leafy greens and herbs (we are baffled that people pay a premium at the supermarket for herbs that are easy to grow at home).

The look or aesthetic

Aesthetics play a crucial role in the success of the home veggie patch, and there is a real benefit to defining your growing space. An attractive and defined patch will draw you and your family towards it as well as give you ownership of your endeavours; an uninviting patch, on the other hand, will help you become an even better procrastinator.

As well as creating something that looks good, you want your veggie patch to fit in with the landscaping style of your garden. If your garden has an informal layout, it could be complemented by a couple of recycled apple crates. Conversely, cottage gardens are better suited to a more formal layout of brick edging and defined herb beds. If you're constructing your garden out of pots and containers, try to keep the materials and colours consistent; a garden full of small, mismatched pots will look cluttered, and the work of a professional pot-hoarder!

Raised beds

A number of our clients opt for raised garden beds, which have quickly become a 'must have' in the edible garden scene. And what a scene! Raised garden beds are the perfect infrastructure for starting a veggie patch; not only do they look good and help define the growing space, they also have practical benefits, such as providing good drainage and an ergonomic height from which to tend the veggies. For more on raised garden beds, see page 14.

Trellising and espaliering

Growing food vertically helps conserve growing space, so encourage your creeping plants to grow up fences or individual trellis towers. Cucumbers, beans, tomatoes, pumpkins and peas are all vegetables that can be grown on some form of climbing trellis; if you have little space, you can still attempt to grow these species. Creeping plants can also be companion plants, providing useful shade for other crops.

Espaliering is a technique used to train a fruit tree to grow flat against a wall or trellis. Nearly all fruit trees can be espaliered; however, some types really benefit from espaliering. Citrus varieties — such as lemon, lime and orange — will love absorbing the heat when trained against a north- or west-facing wall.

These two growing techniques not only serve the practical function of space saving but can also make your veggie patch a feature, in the same breath putting to rest the old school idea that edible gardening is messy and unsightly.

Watering

The success of your veggie patch is dependent on the availability of water, so your number one priority is to ensure the water supply is adequate. As you cannot (and should not, for that matter) rely on mains water alone, you'll need to consider installing a small rainwater tank. Tanks come in many styles and sizes, and the most economical solution is to place it near a downpipe to reduce the cost of plumbing. Recycling grey water from your washing machine is another useful method of supplementing your watering needs, as it is more regularly available than rainwater.

If you live in an apartment or have only a small garden with no room for a water tank, collect grey water from the shower or bath — either place a bucket in the shower

recess, or use it to carry used bath water out to the garden. If you bathe daily (and you should), you will have a constant supply of re-useable water for your garden.

Whether you use mains water, rainwater or grey water, the most efficient way to water your vegetables is via a drip hose system. Installing one of these in your veggie patch should be a given — see page 27 for instructions. Drip systems use water more efficiently (penetrating directly to the roots, where the plant uses it), and they don't wet the leaves like conventional sprays, which increases the plant's susceptibility to fungal diseases.

Pollinators and predators

Your veggies will need bees and other insects to pollinate them. Insects and birds that help counteract pests are also worthwhile, so you will need to lure these good guys to your vegetable patch. Your aim is to create a vibrant mini-ecosystem that beneficial insects and birds will find simply irresistible.

Your existing garden plants and trees will go some way to attracting them, but you can heighten the appeal by incorporating fruit trees, fragrant flowers and herbs into your garden layout. Fruit trees are especially useful, as they can also create natural shade barriers. Even more significantly, they can be used for delicious jam spreads, neighbourhood bartering schemes and domestic food fights.

Companion planting and crop rotation

Companion planting is the process of growing two plants together for the distinct benefit of one crop or the mutual benefit of both. One plant may provide shade for a smaller, more tender plant, or emit a scent that attracts pollinators or wards off pests, or create any other positive effect that is noticeable but perhaps hard to explain. When deciding on your planting layout, grow mutually beneficial companion plants together to optimise your crop.

While some relationships in companion planting can be scientifically proven — for example, the crop rotation practice of planting tomatoes after a broad bean crop, whereby the beans naturally 'fix' or replenish the soil with nitrogen that the tomato crop needs in spades to thrive — other known companion plant relationships are not so easy to determine. Why do onions and strawberries love each other so much? Answer — they just do.

Much of the companion planting know-how we use today has resulted from centuries of growing and the knowledge acquired through nothing more than trial and error. Sometimes it's best not to ask questions and just take the lead from the people who have done this before.

Note that companion planting is hard to practise in a limited space. The main rule about companion planting in small gardens is to encourage biodiversity by planting a range of different plants rather than creating a monoculture.

Deciding what to plant

Ensure you plant what you love and will eat; a vegetable grown without being eaten may as well have been a pretty flower instead.

Within your veggie patch, it's important to use the space wisely. Focus on planting crops that are fast-growing and will rotate easily, and build up your confidence with successful endeavours rather than risk potential heartbreaks. One client invested their heart and soul in growing a gigantic globe artichoke that occupied almost an entire veggie patch. It took a whole year to mature and then mysteriously died, without producing a single edible flower!

You need to be aware that some vegetables are simply not suited to growing in small spaces. For example, say you insisted on growing your favourite food, sweetcorn, in your tiny, 0.5 m² patch. Now as sweetcorn should be grown in groups of 20 plants or more to ensure good pollination, for all your endeavour and dedication you would be rewarded with nothing more than frustration, anger and probably a great reluctance to growing anything, ever again.

Go organic

It's a 'no-brainer' that composting and worm-farming should be integrated into the design of your veggie patch. When you're in the kitchen and sorting though the household rubbish, you'll be amazed at what is either recyclable or compostable. Engaging in smart waste disposal practices will not only help you create some useful garden fertiliser, it will also reduce your carbon footprint. Worm-farming is fun, and dirty enough to lure your kids into helping with the process.

Whether composting or worm-farming, be sure to choose a spot that is well-shaded. Worms hate being baked alive, and your compost pile creates its own heat for the composting process. A spot out of sight is also advisable — let's face it, composting and worm-farming are average-looking at best, and to date we have not seen a system that turns heads.

The 'out of sight' spot, more importantly, needs to be relatively accessible to the place you produce most of your useable waste, usually your kitchen. If the location of your compost unit or worm farm doesn't facilitate easy and regular use, it will be out of mind as well as out of sight.

UNDERSTANDING YOUR SOIL

Soil is the single most important component of a vegetable garden. It's the conduit of all good things necessary for the survival and healthy development of plants. Understanding the vital role soil plays is part of any basic education in gardening. Welcome to Soil 101!

Soil is a living, evolving thing. The way it has been formed over time will contribute to its ability to support life, while the plants and organisms that have lived and died in it will affect its fertility. And then there's what we, as gardeners, do to it.

Types of soil

There are three common types of soil — silt, clay and sand.

The ability of different types of soil to retain moisture and support life is affected by their particle size. Sand has the largest particle size, and therefore struggles to hold moisture, while clay has the finest, and tends to become waterlogged.

The ideal soil type is sandy loam, which combines the strengths of each type of soil to create a super soil. Made up of a mix of 40% sand, 40% silt and 20% clay, it is able to retain nutrition as well as to drain water. However, growing vegetables successfully takes more than purchasing the perfect sandy loam from your garden centre.

Any soil you purchase is largely devoid of constructive life. It is your responsibility to create and nurture life within it by adding compost, fertiliser or worm castings. Feed your soil, and you'll feed your crops. Over time, your soil will improve as it becomes a living organism, better able to accumulate and transmit the nutrients essential for the growth of your plants. If possible, it's a good idea to incorporate the soil you currently have in your garden, as it will contain worms and other living organisms that can only help your veggie patch.

Compaction of your soil is also something that requires consideration, particularly for the gardener using smaller containers and pots to grow food. If this happens to be you, be sure to keep your soil friable. One way of achieving this is to incorporate high levels of organic matter in your mix; this creates beneficial air pockets in the soil (yes, soil needs to breathe too!) and also feed your plants as it breaks down. Perlite, a naturally occurring volcanic substance, can also be used to prevent soil compaction and help the soil to drain well.

When growing edibles in pots, it is worth spending the money and getting a good quality organic potting mix. Many of the cheaper mixes have very little nutrient content and will provide you with very poor crops. If you can, purchase a potting mix that is certified by the BFA (Biological Farmers of Australia) or NASAA (National Association for Sustainable Agriculture Australia).

Nutrition

The three main elements of nutrition that your plants require are nitrogen, potassium and phosphorus.

Fertilisers largely comprise these three elements, which will be displayed on the packet label in values of N (nitrogen), P (phosphorus) and K (potassium). Plants also require trace elements such as zinc, iron, magnesium and calcium, which contribute to their overall health. These trace elements are present in sufficient dosages in your mulches, compost and manures, so don't overly concern yourself with them. Magnesium is the only one worth mentioning, as a deficiency will make leaves turn yellow.

Each of these three main elements is useful at different stages of a plant's growing life. Generally, as your plant develops and matures, its requirements of these elements will shift from nitrogen to potassium.

> Nitrogen (N) helps initiate and then sustain healthy plant growth.

> Phosphorus (P) helps store energy in the plant, assisting it to mature by promoting root, flower and seed development.

> Potassium (K) assists fruit quality, contributing to better taste, less acidity and thicker skins.

pH levels

Maintaining an appropriate pH level in your soil is just as important as ensuring plant nutrition. The pH level dictates how plants are able to absorb the nutrients as well as the activity of micro-organisms within it. Most vegetables prefer a slightly acidic soil, within the

pH range of 5.0 to 7.0, but each vegetable will have an optimal pH level they prefer. The optimal pH level for each individual vegetable is provided in our A to Z edible plant list.

The natural pH balance of your soil is affected by climatic conditions. Dry, arid conditions generally contribute to higher pH levels, while prolific rain will help reduce it. Not surprisingly, much of Australia's soil tends to be acidic. The best way to neutralise the pH level of your soil is to add compost and organic matter, which will provide nutrition at the same time. We don't want to sound like a couple of dietitians, but a balanced diet will keep your soil regular.

In extreme cases, and preferably as a last resort, you can use other additives that will in time restore the pH of your soil. If your soil is highly acidic, lime can be added to increase the pH, while alkaline soils may require an application of aluminium sulphate or sulphur to help restore the balance. In these cases, it is critical to get the mix right, as additives can have a long-term effect on your soil and its pH. For this reason, it's best to stick with organic matter and compost.

The ability of the pH level of your soil to change is affected by its composition. Sandy soils absorb materials rapidly and therefore restore pH faster, while clay-based soils are slow to react.

Organic solutions

There are many ways you can satisfy the nutrient needs of your plants and restore the pH level of your soil without using inorganic fertilisers.

Fresh chook manure

> **Pros** A high source of nitrogen, fresh chook manure also contains potassium and phosphorus. Chook poo can also help increase the acidity of your soil.

> **Cons** It will burn your plants if you apply it directly.

> **How to use** A few weeks prior to planting, dig fresh chook manure, along with pea straw or lucerne hay, through the soil to a depth of 20–30 cm, and allow it to settle and break down.

Pelletised chicken manure

> **Pros** This rich, slow-release form of chook manure can be directly applied without fear of burning.

> **How to use** Apply directly to the surface while planting and water in. You can also dig it through the soil to a depth of 20–30 cm immediately prior to planting.

Horse manure

> **Pros** It contains good levels of nitrogen (about half that of chook manure).

> **Cons** It will burn your plants if applied directly. Be wary of collecting horse poo from racing stables as their horses are regularly wormed, so their manure will affect the worms in your garden.

> **How to use** A few weeks prior to planting, dig horse manure through the soil to a depth of 20–30 cm. As it can contain undigested weeds, composting is recommended.

Cow manure

> **Pros** A source of good bacteria for your soil, cow manure can be added without fear of burning your

plants. It contains the same level of nitrogen as horse manure.

> **How to use** Apply directly while planting.

Green manure

> **Pros** This is usually a leguminous crop, such as broad beans and peas, which is reintegrated into the soil to provide useful nitrogen for the next season's crop. They can also be grown to suppress weeds when the patch is laying idle.

> **How to use** Two to three weeks prior to planting your spring crop, plough it through your soil, to a depth of 20–30 cm. Integrate the green manure plant before flowering to provide the best level of nitrogen.

Compost

> **Pros** Rich in organic matter, compost contains high levels of nitrogen.

> **How to use** When preparing the veggie garden each season, dig it through the soil to a depth of 20–30 cm. You can also add it to the surface around your plants when they require nutrition. Water in after such an application.

Worm castings

> **Pros** An excellent soil conditioner, worm castings promote good bacterial growth in the soil and allow the plants to process the nutrients within.

> **How to use** After planting, sprinkle worm castings around the base of veggies.

Blood and bone

> **Pros** It's rich in nitrogen and phosphorus.

> **How to use** A couple of weeks prior to planting, dig it through the soil to a depth of 20–30 cm.

Potash

> **Pros** It's the best source of potassium for the garden.

> **How to use** Add potash before plants start to flower, or mix it in with blood and bone and add it as a total plant fertiliser prior to planting. When adding potash to flowering plants, it's best to use the liquid form, which can be applied with a watering can.

Fish emulsion

> **Pros** This soil conditioner contains high levels of nitrogen and helps promote good bacterial growth within the soil.

> **How to use** Dilute the fish emulsion with water and, once a fortnight, apply it with a watering can over the veggie garden.

Seaweed extract

> **Pros** A fantastic conduit for plants to absorb necessary nutrients, it helps protect plants from soil-borne diseases.

> **How to use** Dilute seaweed extract with water and, once a fortnight, apply it with a watering can over the veggie garden.

Wood ash

> **Pros** Wood ash provides a valuable source of potassium and also reduces soil acidity.

> **How to use** Dig wood ash through your soil before planting your crop. But don't use wood ash where you plan to grow potatoes.

Garden lime or dolomite lime

> **Pros** These raise the pH level of the soil and provide valuable trace elements, including calcium and magnesium.

> **How to use** In autumn, dig one or the other through the soil to a depth of at least 30 cm and allow it to work through the soil over winter. We tend to use dolomite lime, as it contains a higher level of magnesium; however, both will do the same job of neutralising acidic soil.

Aluminium sulphate/sulphur

> **Pros** Over time this will reduce the pH level of your soil.

> **How to use** In autumn, dig it through the soil to a depth of at least 30 cm. This will allow it to work through the soil over winter.

Test the pH level of your soil

Knowing the pH level of your soil will help you to work out what is required to improve your soil and suit your growing needs. Determining the pH level is as simple as a home pregnancy test — the complications lie in the results!

Maintaining an ideal pH level is an ongoing project, which you should assess and act upon seasonally. Don't 'shock' your soil by overdoing things with pH-altering materials. Working out how your soil reacts to these materials is something that takes time, so keep it simple.

Follow these easy steps to determine the pH level of your soil, then adjust it to suit your growing needs.

Here's what you will need:

> pH test kit

1 Take a sample of soil and place it on a non-porous surface (usually provided in the kit). Mix the solution with the soil.

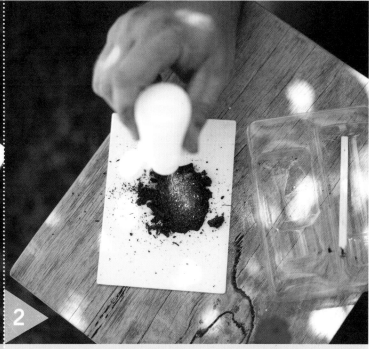

2 Sprinkle with the powder and wait for the colour to form.

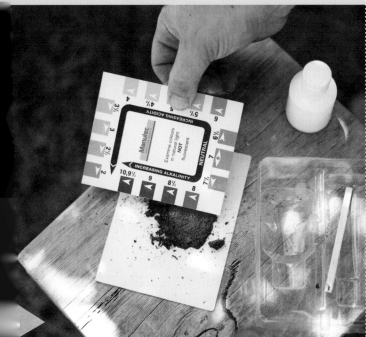

Purple indicates an alkaline soil. If your soil is alkaline, you will need to reduce the pH level by adding organic matter or compost. For severe cases, use small quantities of aluminium sulphate at the change of season.

4 Yellow indicates acidic, which means you will need to increase the pH level. Try adding wood ash during the growing season, or well-decomposed chook manure at the change of season. For severe cases, incorporate small doses of lime at the change of the growing season.

RAISED GARDEN BEDS

Many gardening enthusiasts believe that raised garden beds are essential for growing vegetables, and we wouldn't argue. If constructed soundly, using the right materials, your raised garden bed will provide a focal point for your garden as well as the ideal infrastructure for growing vegetables at home.

There are a number of advantages to growing your vegetables in a raised garden bed, particularly in an urban environment, so when your curious neighbour peeps over the fence and asks, 'Hey there, why are you building raised garden beds?', you can respond with one or all of the following points.

> They allow me to tend my vegetables at an ergonomic height.

> They allow me to import good quality soil.

> There are few compaction issues.

> They remove competition for water from the more established plants in my garden.

> They help my veggies chase sunlight by elevating the growing level.

> They always ensure good drainage.

> They look great, provide me with a focal point for my vegetable growing and, look, they can double up as seating too!

While a raised garden bed is typically thought of as a timber box, 2.4 m by 1.2 m, anything that allows you to import soil and elevates the level of your growing space can be considered a raised garden bed. We recycle wooden crates we source from apple orchards and make them into raised garden beds (see page 21). Containers and pots are smaller examples.

It is important to note that many inner city areas have been contaminated by previous agricultural or industrial practices — another reason why we recommend building raised garden beds. If you wish to grow directly into existing soil but are concerned about your area, get your soil tested — contact your local council for advice.

When installing any raised garden bed, it's a good idea to let your new soil settle for at least a few days, up to a week, before planting. This will allow it to establish an even and more veggie-friendly temperature, and for the soil to find its compaction density.

Size

When planning the width of your raised garden bed, be aware that you will need to access the crops while standing outside the bed — climbing onto it defeats the purpose of building one in the first place.

Width

Go for 1.5 m in width as a maximum, and make it accessible from either side. If you're constructing your garden bed against a fence, you will need to reduce the width to no more than 1 m wide. Confining the patch to the perimeter of your available area is a good way to maximise your outdoor space and also gives you the chance to grow climbing crops up a trellis secured to the fence.

Length

This is totally up to you and the space you have at hand.

Height

Height plays an important role in raised garden beds. A garden bed that's 60 cm high is easier to tend, chases more sunlight, allows better drainage and soil preparation, reduces water competition, is more comfortable to sit on and, according to some gardeners, looks better than a bed that's only 40 cm high.

Cost and time are determining factors here — the higher the bed, the more materials required and the more it costs to build. Weigh up those factors, then choose the height of your garden bed accordingly.

Materials

Choose building materials that are easy to work with and suit the style of your existing landscaping. You also need to ensure that the materials you choose are safe and won't leach chemicals into your soil, compromising the safety of what you grow and intend to eat. For example, pine timber, abbreviated to CCA, is treated with arsenic to prolong its life. We don't believe arsenic and strawberries make a great mix.

Ninety-nine per cent of the raised beds we install for our clients are constructed from timber. The following timbers are suitable for building your raised garden bed, with our thoughts on value for money, longevity and their aesthetic appeal. The availability of timbers will vary from state to state, depending on where they are produced.

Cypress pine

A dense, beautifully knotted timber, cypress pine possesses a natural oil that makes it resilient to termites (white ants). It is good to work with and reasonable value for money. Finding grades of timber that are appropriate for building raised garden beds will be your challenge. Cypress pine is the Little Veggie Patch Co's timber of choice.

Red gum (new)

Red gum has traditionally been the 'it' timber for raised vegetable gardens. Widespread availability, density of timber and value for money made it particularly appealing, and it was our timber of choice when we started out in 2007. However, it has since become much maligned due to its propensity to bow and warp as it dries out. Red gum production is being phased out, and in a few years it will be hard to come by.

Red gum (recycled)

Aged, recycled railway sleepers will not warp or bow, and are cut at a grade so thick they will last nearly a lifetime, creating an authentic-looking vegetable garden. However, be wary — they are susceptible to termites, and are so heavy they will substantially lower your morale when you attempt to pick the first one up!

Jarrah and merbau

These dense, natural timbers are very good to work with. They age well but are costly in comparison to the alternatives.

Tassie oak

A dense, natural timber that's also very good to work with, ages sensationally. If we could afford it, we would build everything out of Tassie oak, but let's face it, building an outdoor vegetable garden out of Tassie oak timber is probably a little excessive.

Eco timber (ACQ variety)

Eco timber, or ACQ, is the sibling of evil brother CCA-treated pine. It is easy to handle and work with, and safe to use in your raised garden beds. The most cost-effective and eco-friendly timber for the job, it is becoming more readily available.

Recycled print cartridges

This 'timber' is made from recycled print cartridges and is completely safe and good to work with. Because of its flex, it will require bracing at smaller box sizes than the other timbers to stop it from bulging, and aesthetically there are a few question marks.

HOW TO
Build a basic raised garden bed

Building a raised garden bed is not difficult, and it is even more straightforward if you use the correct tools. For this job you will require:

> rake
> timber sleepers (200 x 50 mm):
  6 × 2.4 m (lengths)
  3 × 2.4 m (widths)
  2 × 2.4 m (bracing uprights)
> tape measure
> pencil
> circular saw
> spirit level
> drill
> timber screws (75 mm)
> set square
> shovel
> wheelbarrow
> 1.75m³ soil blend

Using a garden rake, level the area on which you will construct the raised garden bed.

Prepare your lengths, widths and uprights, cutting to exact size where necessary with a circular saw. Be sure to measure twice, cut once! Use a set square to ensure all cuts are perfectly square.

You should have the following pieces:
6 x 2.4 m (lengths)
6 x 1.2 m (widths)
6 x 0.6 m (bracing uprights)

Note: there will be some offcuts.

Line up 3 lengths evenly, position a bracing upright at either end (with an overhang of 50 mm), one in the centre and secure using 6 screws per upright. Repeat with the remaining 3 lengths and 3 uprights. You should now have 2 length-walls.

5

Position your first length-wall. Use a spirit level to ensure it is level and standing perfectly upright.

6

Starting from the bottom, attach 3 widths to the length-wall, using 2 screws to attach each width. With one length-wall and one width-wall in place, you're halfway there!

7

Position and attach the remaining length-wall, and then attach the 3 remaining widths to complete your raised garden bed.

8

Fill the bed with a good quality soil blend and allow the contents to settle in for a few days before deciding which seeds and seedlings to add.

NO-DIG (LAZY) GARDENING

While a no-dig garden could be dubbed the lazy person's garden, it is also the smart person's garden.

A no-dig garden is created by layering organic matter such as straw, compost, worm castings and manure as a substitute for soil. As the contents decompose, they feed your plants with an array of necessary nutrients.

There is no need for backbreaking tilling, and if you get the mix of your organic matter right, there is no need to supplement with fertilisers. For this reason, no-dig gardening is synonymous with organic gardening. One early proponent of the technique, Japanese farmer-philosopher, Masanobu Fukuoka, even coined the term 'Do-nothing Farming' — no doubt attracting the interest of every person who likes getting something for nothing.

A no-dig garden goes hand in hand with your raised garden bed — in fact it goes inside your raised garden bed. It can be constructed over any spot that receives sufficient sunlight for growing vegetables — over a patch of dead grass, an old garden bed, apartment balcony, even the traditional concrete slab.

As the organic layers break down to feed your vegetables, the level of your no-dig garden will be reduced, so the only maintenance required is a top-up of ingredients (for example, some compost) when necessary — usually as the season's crops finish.

No tilling

The biggest advantage of a no-dig garden is not having to till or dig over the soil. In standard gardening tilling is required to aerate the soil while introducing compost and manure. However, it can be harmful to the health of the soil, as it disturbs its structure and displaces nutrients and the life within. It can also provoke dormant weed seeds into life and activate a weed problem.

In a no-dig garden, however, the layers of organic matter are left undisturbed, and with the help of worms and microbes, a vibrant and nutrient-rich soil structure is created.

Materials

Because no-dig gardens replace soil with layers of lighter, compostable materials, your container will hold less than half the weight of a standard raised garden bed. This will increase the possibilities for the apartment gardener, who may be restricted by load bearings on balconies or terraces, effectively doubling the amount of veggies they can grow.

Less weight also means you can be a little more creative when it comes to constructing a no-dig garden. We've seen many examples of 'thrown together' no-dig gardens that incorporate whatever materials people happen to have lying around their homes. Old bricks stacked without concrete binding, logs, even bales of straw can be used to create the walls. Recycled materials seem to suit this style of gardening, reinforcing the idea of 'Do-nothing Gardening' by creating something out of seemingly nothing.

Increasingly, we've been sourcing crates from an apple grower out of Melbourne and using them for veggie patches. Recycled apple crates make an ideal space for no-dig layering, allowing a depth of 60 cm for the layering. As they are made from non-treated timber, there is no concern about harmful chemicals leaching into your growing medium, and the price of an apple crate is a fraction of what it would cost to build a similar-sized raised garden bed from scratch. If you're a newcomer to veggie gardening, creating a no-dig garden in a recycled apple crate is an ideal starting point. It allows you to determine if growing vegetables is in fact for you, without you investing too much time and money.

Ideas on how to set up a no-dig garden — including what materials to use, how much and in what order, and what colour underpants you should be wearing when preparing the garden — will vary from source to source. So while there are no fixed rules on setting up a no-dig garden, we too have our own proven formula that we stubbornly stand by.

While the recycled crates we use are 60 cm in depth, anything deeper than 30 cm will provide adequate depth for good layering and an effective no-dig garden.

Setting up over lawn or an existing garden bed

If you are setting up your garden over a lawn or garden bed, we recommend you start with a 0.5–1.0 cm layer of wet newspaper and cardboard. This will help suppress any weeds or grass sprouting through your no-dig garden and will, in turn, decompose and feed your soil.

This is how the Little Veggie Patch Co sets up a no-dig garden in our recycled apple crates. You will require:

> 1 recycled apple crate 1.2 (L) x 1.2 (W) x 0.6 (D) m
> wheelbarrow
> shovel
> 1 bale plain straw
> 1 small bag of slow-release organic fertiliser (pellet form)
> ½ m³ mushroom compost
> 1 bale lucerne hay or pea straw
> 15-litre bag worm castings

1

Lay 20 cm of straw (one bale) on the base of the crate. This will act as a filler and filter for drainage rather than as a source of nutrients for your vegetables.

2

Incorporate a few handfuls of slow-release organic fertiliser. This is the stinky stuff, but if you really set your mind to it, it could be mistaken for Belgian dark chocolate.

3

Add 10 cm of mushroom compost (2 wheelbarrows' worth), spread and compact down.

4

Add 10 cm of either lucerne hay or pea straw, and then incorporate a few handfuls of slow-release organic fertiliser.

Add 20 cm of mushroom compost (4 wheelbarrows), spread and compact down.

6

Incorporate a handful of a slow-release organic fertiliser to the surface.

Add the bag of worm castings as a conduit for the nutrients to your plants.

8

Because this is a fertile and quite raw mix, it is best to allow the contents to settle in for a few days before deciding what seeds and seedlings to plant.

THE IMPORTANCE OF WATER

Living in Australia we are aware, more than most, of water's importance in the garden and in our lives in general. Lasting drought and water restrictions have made cursing the lack of water a habit. Inbuilt mechanisms in some people force them to blurt out 'How we needed this rain!' even after prolonged wet periods — an involuntarily reaction akin to closing your eyes when you sneeze. However, what it all highlights is that, in this country, water in the garden is an issue that needs careful consideration.

The first thing you should realise is that plants are 80% water, and therefore need it to survive. Having a regular supply of water that is administered intelligently and efficiently will optimise your growing endeavours.

Sources of water

When it comes to supply, there are four ways to source water.

1 Mains supply

Most city dwellers rely on mains water to grow their vegetables. This is easy but lazy, and water restrictions mean that mains water use is not always sufficient.

2 Tank water

When it's possible, supplementing your watering by collecting rainfall is a no-brainer and a worthy, sustainable practice. Tanks come in a range of sizes, shapes and styles to suit all households and budgets. These days when it rains, it really does pour, so having a tank is the best way to catch nature's gift. To work out the amount of water you can potentially collect, measure the surface area of the roof you are collecting from and multiply it by the annual rainfall.

For example, a 100 m^2 roof in Melbourne (with an annual rainfall of approximately 600 mm) will collect 100 m^2 × 600 = 60,000 litres of water.

3 Grey water

While tank water relies on rainfall to be useful, we are always using household water that can be recycled and reused on the garden. This type of water is known as grey water (which is any water used to wash, whether it's in the kitchen or the bathroom), and it is safe to use on your vegetable garden as long as you manage the detergents you use. Choose detergents that are readily biodegradable, and avoid those that contain phosphates, bleaches or synthetic fragrances.

Black water is water that contains human waste — for example, that from the toilet. There is some disagreement on whether bath and shower water should be considered black water rather than grey; however, that really depends what you do in the shower.

4 Direct rainfall

Rainfall can meet your watering needs for much of the year. During some winters, irrigation can go almost unused and we can have the problem of too much water. Likewise in summer, particularly in the northern states, rains can provide an overabundance of water that should be observed and managed.

Drip hose watering

Watering the veggie patch used to be done by exciting and inefficient sprays that significantly wasted water if the morning breeze was up; you could even dance under them. These days, brown, bland drip hose is the preferred and sometimes only legal method of watering, and rightly so.

Drip hose is poly tubing that has filtered holes every 30 cm, each hole releasing approximately 3 L of water every hour. Drip hose penetrates the water directly into the soil, where it is used up completely by the plant and living soil organisms. Deeper penetration of the water in the soil encourages roots to travel further for a drink, and therefore promotes stronger root growth. Drip hose watering also reduces the potential of pest and disease problems that are heightened when plant leaves are left wet after watering. It also means it is possible to give your plants a drink on extremely hot days without fear of burning their foliage.

With a drip hose installed (as shown in the activity on page 27), set it to water once a week during the winter and twice during summer for a run time of 20 minutes each water. This will satisfy the watering requirements of your established plants. Set the system to come on in the morning, allowing the plants to use the water during the day, when it is needed most. This also means the surface of the patch should be dry at night, reducing the chance of pests striking.

When installing a drip system, make sure you use a pressure reducer to regulate the flow of water in the line and prevent fittings from breaking free under pressure. Also include a flush valve and air-release vacuum, which will clear the lines of any grit and air pockets, respectively.

Watering seeds and seedlings

When your veggie seeds and seedlings are establishing, they will require supplementary watering for the tiny root growths that a drip hose system can miss. To avoid damaging the seedlings or dislodging your seeds, use a gentle fan spray on your hose or a watering can with a fan spray, and water in the mornings. Most juvenile seedlings will require regular watering — leafy greens daily and other veggies 3–4 times a week for the first 2–3 weeks.

Soil composition

Your soil's composition affects the way it holds and drains water. If it is heavily clay-based, water will have trouble penetrating it to be used effectively by plants. Instead, the water will pool or saturate at the surface, causing rotting and disease. Sandy soils hold water like a sieve and dry out rapidly. Finding the right balance in your soil is critical.

If your soil is at the sandy end of the spectrum, the best way to improve its water-holding capacity is to add organic matter. Methodically adding compost and manure to your veggie garden at the turn of the season, or when your plants demand their tonic, not only improves the nutrient value of the soil but also incorporates coarser and more water-absorbent particles into its structure. If you are faced with a cloggy clay soil, organic matter will also help it to rebalance and introduce life to the soil that will help it break away from its clay origins. Sometimes the use of lime or gypsum is also recommended to help accelerate this process.

Mulching

One practice that will improve your soil's water retention is mulching, which involves covering the topsoil with a layer of material that helps suppress weeds and reduce evaporation. Theoretically, mulch is anything that does those two jobs, so it can be made up of rocks, coarse woodchips, fine bark or hay/straw. For vegetable gardens, however, we want our mulch to feed our veggies and provide valuable organic matter, so we recommend using pea straw or lucerne hay and applying it to a thickness of 3–5 cm. Keep the mulch a few centimetres away from the plants' stems, as it can cause stem rot.

Initially, the mulch will reduce evaporation and allow the plants more time to use the water while simultaneously suppressing competing weeds. Later on in its life cycle, the lucerne or pea straw will break down and decompose, adding valuable nutrients to your soil and in turn improving its water retention.

Ideally we'd like to mulch as soon as the seedlings have been planted; however, when they are newborns and tiny in size, the mulch can be cumbersome to apply without doing damage. You also run the risk of suppressing the growth of your seedlings, treating them as the weeds! Therefore applying the mulch 2–4 weeks after germination is best. Depending on what mulch you use and how quickly it breaks down, you may need to reapply it mid-season, particularly over summer.

Install a drip irrigation system

An automated drip system waters your plants directly at the roots and, unlike conventional fan sprays, does not waste water. As the system operates on a timer, it will also water your crops when you can't, or in the unlikely event that you have something more important to do.

Most of you will have (or should have!) a drip hose in your existing garden beds, so here we will simply add your veggie irrigation to an existing irrigation line – meaning the veggies will get watered at the same time as your other plants. Remember a drip system is predominantly for established veggies (that have similar watering requirements to other non-edible plants) – your seeds and seedlings will require supplementary surface watering when young.

Here is how to set up your own drip watering grid on a veggie patch measuring 2.4 m by 1.2 m.

For this sized system you will need:

> 15 m drip hose

> 6 x 13 mm tees*

> 5 x 13 mm elbows*

> 10 x metal drip hose pegs

> 100-pack of 13 mm ratchet clamps

> small roll of 13 mm black
  poly pipe**

> measuring tape

> multi-grips

> pipe cutters or knife

*   The number of tees and elbows required may vary, depending on the distance the existing irrigation line is from your new veggie patch irrigation system.

** The length of poly pipe will depend on the distance from the veggie bed to your existing system, as this will be your feeder line.

1

2

Before filling your raised bed with soil, place a feeder line (using the poly pipe) that will lead out of your veggie bed towards your existing irrigation drip line. The existing line will be your water supply.

Connect this feeder line to the existing line. When the weather is cold the hose can be quite rigid and hard to attach to the joins. Soaking the hose ends in a cup of hot water for 5–10 seconds befo attaching helps greatly.

3

4

When cutting into the drip hose be careful not to cut too closely to the water release holes or you won't be able to insert your joins; allow at least 2–3 cm.

Affix a ratchet clamp at each join and tighten using a pair of multi-grips.

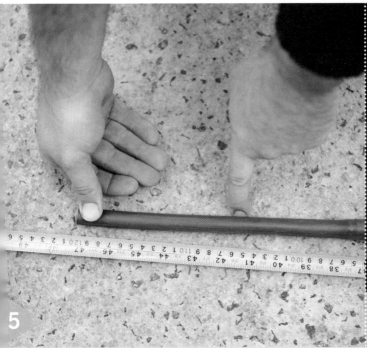

5

Measure the width of the bed and then cut 2 lengths that will be 15 cm shorter at either end. Our width is 1.2 m, so the hose width will be 0.9 m. Measure the length of the bed and then cut 4 lengths that will be 15 cm shorter at either end. Our length is 2.4 m, so the hose length will be 2.1 m.

6

Taking one of the shorter lengths of drip hose, attach an elbow at either end, making sure the outlets are facing the same direction.

Evenly space the two tees through the centre of this length, making cuts and inserting, and making sure the outlets are facing the same direction as the elbows. (Don't worry if you can't insert the tees exactly in the middle if water release holes are in the way – get as close as you can.) Affix a ratchet clamp at every join, using a pair of multi-grips.

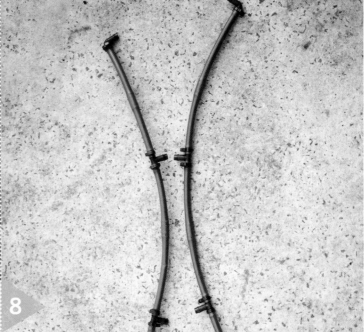

8

Repeat the process for the remaining shorter length of drip hose.

9

Now taking the lengths of drip hose, form your grid by connecting them to both width segments you have made up. Keep the lengths parallel and ensure they do not cross over. Affix a ratchet clamp at every join, using a pair of multi-grips.

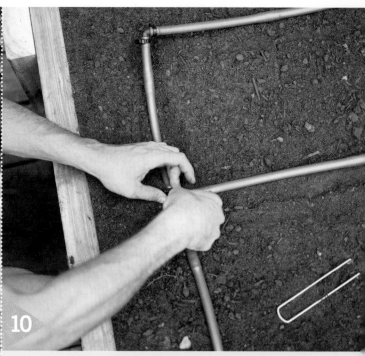

10

Take your grid and position it in the centre of the veggie patch. Fasten it to the soil using metal pegs, using as many as necessary to hold it down.

11

Your grid needs to be connected to the water source, so attach it to the feeder line you have joined to your existing irrigation line. Cut into the line and connect with a tee, remembering to ratchet-clamp all joins. If you do not have an existing irrigation line to connect to, we recommend you enlist the help of an irrigation professional.

Spacing the drip hose evenly throughout the patch will help ensure it is evenly watered. As drip hose is pierced with holes every 30 cm, making our rows 30 cm apart will create an even grid of water.

SOWING YOUR SEEDS

To plant seeds, or seedlings, that is the question... A good number of the part-time, fair-weathered gardening community fall for the lure of planting established seedlings in the misguided belief that they're creating an instantaneous garden without the associated investment of time and effort. No doubt most of us would choose to bypass the first couple of months of parenthood and purchase babies with an immediate personality and more defined features, bringing you two months closer to the possibility of a good night's sleep. While the lure of mature infants seems a disturbed but brilliant idea, the outcome, as with mature seedlings, isn't all it's made out to be.

Growing conditions

The first problem with mature seedlings is that the conditions in which they are grown will most likely differ widely from the conditions in which they will settle. Most seedlings you find at a garden nursery are not locally grown, and therefore not developed to cope with your garden situation. This is never more evident than when you visit a Victorian hardware chain store stocking tomato seedlings in June.

For the first-time veggie grower, whose spirits become buoyed at the sight of a summer crop in the middle of winter, this first outing can be a confidence-shattering experience. And this is the one flaw of the developed infant idea — imagine young Charlie, fresh out of the hospital nursery with its constant supply of food, 24-hour professional care and soft woollen blankets, being thrown into your home with budget constraints and

an unflexible work life, but most cruelly, into itchy, crap polyester. Poor Charlie!

Transplanting

Many plants do not transplant well, and are better sown directly into your veggie patch. Upon transplantation, plants can become stressed, their growth can be stunted, they are more prone to diseases, and may even die. For young Charlie, the shock of moving from wool to polyester may prove too much!

Veggies such as peas, beans, broad beans, radish, beetroot and carrots will all do better when sown directly, rather than being transplanted from punnets.

Seed propagation

Sowing your own seeds will not only save you money on costly seedlings but will also help you develop seedlings that are better adapted to survive in your unique mini-ecosystem. You will in turn become a better carer for your garden, with a better knowledge of the needs of your plants. Seed propagation is also a fun and eye-opening activity that should be part of every kid's early education.

When propagating your own seeds, being aware of their special requirements and the best method of sowing is the best way to ensure that your plants will cope from germination through to maturity. Ideally, save seeds from your own plants or, if you're just starting out, purchase them from a local organic seed supplier.

Temperature

It is important to keep conditions for your seeds as consistent and uniform as possible, as there are ideal soil temperatures for seed germination. Propagating seeds in seed trays or punnets with shallow soil means the soil becomes sensitive to even small changes in temperature. Keeping your seeds in a small greenhouse is the best way to keep temperatures stable, but for most this will not be possible, so keep your seeds indoors at night. This will also help avert potential pest problems, as most pests are active after dark.

Soil mix

Most seeds require a friable, nutrient-rich soil for germination and initial development, allowing the new roots ease of movement and adequate feeding. Well-developed compost or worm castings work best for us, but there are a number of seed-raising mixes that you can purchase from nurseries.

Seed preparation

If your seeds have hard shells, you can assist germination by soaking them overnight before sowing. This helps break down the shell, allowing the new shoot to germinate more easily.

Seed depth

Some seeds require light for germination, while others need darkness. A general rule of thumb for sowing seeds is to plant at a depth that is twice the diameter of the seed. For example, if the seed is 1 cm in diameter, plant it at a depth of 2 cm. You will notice that a lot of seeds are no more than 1 mm in size, so in the case of these seeds, plant at a depth of 0.5–1 cm. This will prevent them from being picked out by birds or blown away.

Watering

Moisture is critical to germination, but you need to keep seeds moist rather than soak them. Seeds require short, regular watering, usually daily. Use a fine fan spray so you don't dislodge them. Some seeds — such as broad beans, beans and peas — are susceptible to rotting in the ground or being picked off by pests that smell the initial decomposition of the seed. These will appreciate an initial soaking when sowed, but little to no water until germination occurs.

Sowing

1 Sowing in situ

This means simply sowing the seeds directly into your veggie garden. You can either scatter them on the surface, which is known as 'broadcasting', or in drills, which is a more methodical process of sowing them in neat rows. The broadcast method is good for sowing seeds of annuals where you want a good cover and have plenty of seeds at hand. Drilling is better when you want a more defined garden, allowing you to walk between your mature plants.

When you have a limited growing area, rows are not always an ideal way to maximise space. Sowing in rows goes back to the agricultural practice of irrigating crops by welling water between the rows, and it is not applicable to inner city gardening. So when space is at a premium, we suggest you use the broadcast method, but you'll need to thin out your seedlings once they have germinated.

For both methods, it is important to prepare the ground. The seeds derive their nutrients from the soil particles, and will find it difficult to germinate when there are large clumps of hard soil. Therefore, you need to prepare a finely tilled soil that is broken into small particles. Remember not to till the soil when it is wet, as it will become hard and clumpy as it dries.

Seed-raising mixes or soil mixes designed for pots or containers will already have a good friable consistency so they don't need to be prepared before sowing.

Broadcast

Simply scatter the seeds over the designated area, gently rake them in and then carefully water. Anything more than a gentle, fine spray will dislodge the seeds from the soil and make them easier prey for hungry birds.

Drilling

Prepare the designated area into rows; to ensure accuracy, you could use a string line and pegs. Create a trench line, with the depth according to the size of the seeds (remember the rule of thumb — the planting depth is twice the seed's diameter), then sow your seeds within it. Cover the seeds by carefully raking the soil back into the trench, firming down gently, then water in.

When drilling in rows, sprinkle smaller seeds evenly along the trench line by rubbing them between your thumb and index/middle fingers as you go. A helpful technique for sowing smaller seeds is to mix your seeds with coarse sand, making it easier to sow them evenly. Plant larger seeds such as peas or beans individually, spaced evenly a few centimetres apart.

Seeds that have been sown by either the broadcast or the drill method will generally need to be thinned out to give them room in which to grow. Do this by removing the unwanted seedlings once they have germinated, perhaps giving them away to friends or neighbours. If you are disposing of the thinnings, add them to your compost bin, and don't leave the plants to decompose on the surface of your veggie patch, as this may attract pests.

2 Sowing in seed trays

Seeds can be grown in trays, either outside, indoors or in a greenhouse. When sowing in this fashion, fill the tray with a coarse soil blend, compost or worm castings, and firm gently. We find compost is best, as it is a pure blend and you can be assured that whatever germinates in the trays will be only your intended seeds.

Depending on the size of the trays and the seeds you are using, you can choose to sow the seeds broadcast, in rows or singly. For example, we broadcast our lettuce seeds, sow beetroot in rows, and plant broad bean seeds singly.

When using such small quantities of soil or compost, it is a good idea to moisten the soil before sowing to prevent the seeds from washing away during their first watering. Another trick is to cover the trays with dampened sheets of newspaper after sowing, thus retaining the moisture and keeping the soil temperature constant.

You can also sow seeds in seed trays with a number of individual cells in them. In this method, we generally sow 2 seeds per cell, in case one fails to germinate. If both seeds germinate, you will need to thin out to allow the remaining seed to develop properly. Using individual cells allows the seed to grow into a mature seedling before being transplanted, which helps with some varieties such as members of the brassica family — for example, broccoli, cauliflower and cabbage.

You can also recycle household waste items such as egg cartons to perform the same function as purchased seed trays with individual cells. More importantly, the cells of the egg cartons can be broken off and buried directly into the patch. The material will quickly decompose and allow the roots to pass through the cardboard, reducing stress on the plant when transplanting.

3 Sowing in individual pots

Much like sowing seeds in individual cells, you can also sow seeds in individual pots (such as jiffy pots). This allows the seedlings to become established plants before transplanting. We do this where seeds may be at a premium, such as your favourite 'Black Russian' tomatoes, or for plants such as capsicum, which typically become stressed when transplanted at a young age.

Use a coarse soil blend, compost or worm castings as the growing medium and follow the rule of thumb for seed depth (see page 32). As with sowing in small cells, sow 2 seeds per pot in case one fails to germinate. If both sprout, cull one carefully.

You can also make individual newspaper pots by moulding the paper to the pot size you wish to use. Look up 'making newspaper pots' on YouTube to see how easy it is. When the seedling is ready to transplant in the patch, plant your newspaper pot directly into the desired position.

Propagate peas

Propagating peas is something we look forward to — another opportunity to improve on last year's crop and taste some new varieties.

We'll show you how to sow pea seeds in individual seed cells. For this activity you will require:

> toilet roll tubes

> seed-raising mix

> 50–100 pea seeds

> watering can (with fan spray)

1 Cut the toilet roll tubes in half and place on a tray.

2 Fill the tubes with seed-raising mix and firm down gently.

Vater the mix to ensure all ingredients are moist and, using the tip of our index finger, create a hole in each tube to a depth of 2–3 cm.

4 Place 2 pea seeds in each hole.

5

Sprinkle more seed-raising mix into the tubes and gently firm down.

6

Water thoroughly with a fan spray. The seeds shouldn't require further watering until germination, unless conditions are particularly warm.

7

Once the seeds have germinated, you may need to thin them out so that only one seedling remains in each cell. Do this by gently removing the excess seedling.

8

After 2–3 weeks, your seedlings will be ready to be planted in their designated spot in the veggie garden, toilet roll tubes and all.

SAVING YOUR SEEDS

'When my Italian grandparents decided to move from southern Italy to central Western Australia (something that was considered clinically insane back then), they packed up the bare essentials and shipped out.

My mother was barely 11 years old, but she remembers trying to force her favourite toy into the heart of the suitcase, only to find that the safest and most valuable space was already occupied. If the boat capsized and all their luggage was lost overboard, only this small pocket of possessions had a chance of surviving. So, what do you think lay in the heart of the suitcase? Photographs? Identification documents? Family heirlooms? No. Inside a jar, inside a jar, inside a jar lay Nonno's finest tomato seeds.

That story tells me worlds about the relationship my Nonno had with his land and his food (particularly tomatoes), and it helps me to identify with where I have come from, and my family's roots — an incredible journey through post-World War II Italy to a gold mine in Kalgoorlie, Western Australia, a brief stopover in Papua New Guinea, into a truly Australian family with infinite opportunities. The journey of my Nonno's seeds is just as incredible.

Just where and when my Nonno's tomato seeds began their journey is unclear, and seeking answers gets me no closer to discovering their origins, but there is no truer form of Darwinism and the survival of the fittest principle than with seed saving.'

MP

Seed saving is something that farmers and home growers have done for centuries, both out of necessity and for the betterment of their crop. Each year they would collect and save seeds from open-pollinated varieties of vegetables, herbs and flowers for sowing in the following season. Over time, the crops grown in their fields were those that had evolved and thrived in the local conditions, giving them superior hardiness, yield and taste. Open pollination refers to the pollination of a plant's flower via wind, insect, bird or any other animal.

Over the last several decades there has been a shift towards purchasing seeds from commercial seed suppliers. Such seeds are hybrid or cloned varieties that may be sterile or, more commonly, fail to produce seeds that have the same genetic makeup as the parent plant, increasing our dependency on commercial seed suppliers. Widespread reliance on these hybrid and cloned seeds is negating the process of evolution, as they are artificially cross-pollinated and designed to produce a higher yield or to meet a particular aesthetic. By design, the second generation seed of the hybrid does not produce a true copy of the original and therefore loses much of its yield potential. Put plainly, the only course of action available to the farmer is to purchase the same seed the following year. It is not by accident that some of the richest companies in the world are agricultural ones.

Widespread use of a relatively few, mass-marketed hybrid seed varieties, in both home gardening and commercial farming, has eliminated many open-pollinated varieties, especially the local variations that were naturally developed. The concern is that our seed gene pool is being eroded and we are heading towards less hardy, more disease-prone plants as our ecosystem's diversity is reduced.

The seed-saving movement is the antagonist of the commercial seed seller, opening a market for the organic farmers and permaculturists who specialise in old or 'heirloom' varieties of seed and their produce.

An heirloom seed is one that has been grown, nurtured, selected and then passed on for the coming generation, much like a family possession that has been passed down from generation to generation. The seed of a heirloom plant is kept pure, meaning it is open-pollinated, and is neither genetically modified nor hybrid.

While hybrid vegetables are designed to suit supermarket chains that rely on aesthetics, weight and yield, the heirloom varieties suit us — the home growers — producing better-tasting veggies that have the ability to adapt to conditions in our own backyards. Heirloom vegetables are now gaining popularity as our taste buds become exposed to 'new' flavours. (Note we say 'new' here with a large dose of sarcasm because the taste of supermarket vegetables is not a true representation of their flavours.)

Seed saving is something that every home gardener should practise. It builds up resistance to the increasing monoculture of seed, plant and food supply, and encourages diversity. Plants, as living things, are constantly adapting to their surroundings. Saving and growing seed, year by year, is taking part in the act of evolution, and that is a very great thing.

In order to save seeds, consider the following.

Records

It is essential to keep good records so you know what is what. Mark the plants in your patch and keep a separate file that records the seed details, such as name, source, planting date and germination rate. Jot down the weather conditions and any event that may affect the outcomes. We suggest investing in a nice notebook so your notes don't get mixed up with the bills and other useless papers.

Selection

Keep a holistic approach to choosing which varieties to save, rather than just choosing the biggest producer of fruit. Consider many factors, including taste, yield, tolerance to weather, tolerance to disease, harvesting times, storage quality and even the characteristics of the soil type around a plant. Success is defined by you, the grower.

Many self-pollinated plant varieties are naturally inbred, so they can be saved from just a few plants. However, depending on the breeding tendencies of the plant, collecting from too few plants may not represent the full diversity of that variety, and so that diversity may be lost. Be sure to check on the characteristics of each variety to ensure safe numbers.

Pollination

Pollination is the process by which pollen is transferred, enabling fertilisation. It occurs when pollen is passed from the male part of the flower (the stamen) to the female part (the stigma) of the flower to make a fertile seed. This process can occur in two ways: cross-pollination or self-pollination. A self-pollinating plant has 'perfect flowers', meaning that they can fertilise themselves, while other plants have 'imperfect flowers' that need to cross-pollinate with other flowers of the same species on another plant.

If you want to save the seeds of a plant that requires cross-pollination, you may wish to isolate the plant from other plants within the species during the time of flowering, otherwise the seeds that are produced may not possess the same genetic makeup as the parent plant, but rather a mix of the two.

It is harder for cross-pollination to occur in built-up areas than in open farm spaces; however, with so many varieties being bred in such a small space, you will sometimes need to use physical barriers to prevent cross-pollination. Caging and bagging are two techniques that mechanically prevent cross-pollination.

Hand-pollination, which is sometimes required to ensure the purity of seeds, involves manually transferring pollen from the stamen of the male flower to the stigma of the female. Methods vary from plant to plant — for example, you can use a paint brush to take pollen from the male to the female flower of a pumpkin plant; likewise, you can transfer the pollen of a tomato plant simply by shaking it gently, mimicking wind pollination.

Planting

To increase your margin of safety, grow more plants than you think is necessary. Remember that you will need to allow more space for each plant as it matures and produces seed, as you don't want them inhibiting each other.

Also remember to devise a good planting plan to keep separate cross-pollinating varieties, that could comtaminate the offspring, or plant at different times so that pollinating times don't cross over.

Harvesting and preparation

When harvesting, always keep the healthiest plant for seeds rather than to eat. The method of saving seeds will vary according to whether the plant produces dry seedcoats, dry fruits or wet fruits.

For plants that produce dry seedcoats (such as lettuce, carrot, cabbage, broccoli, rocket and parsley) cut off the stems with the mature seed pods attached and dry out for a couple of weeks before separating the seeds and storing. Place stockings over the seed pods while they're still on the plant to stop them dropping into the garden bed below once mature.

Harvest dry fruits (such as pumpkin, zucchini, chilli and eggplant) when ripe, open them up and scrape out the seeds, drying them on a plate before transferring to a jar.

Remove the pulp of wet fruit (such as tomato and cucumber) and place in a jar with some water overnight to help dislodge the seeds. There are some who advocate fermenting seeds before sorting them for collection, in order to help kill off disease. Many tomato seed savers store their raw seeds and pulp in a jar for up to a fortnight until a crust of fermentation appears. They then wash it off and dry the seed.

Threshing and separation

Leave non-fruiting plants to flower and develop seed heads, then pick the flowers or seed pod and allow them to dry. Thresh the seeds by using your fingers to break the seeds from the flower head, carefully crushing and removing the seed case from the seeds. Don't apply too much pressure or you'll damage the seed.

Insects or diseases

Applying a hot water treatment to the seeds will ensure that any pest or disease that may be carried by that seed is killed or sterilised. To do this, submerge the seed in water at a constant temperature of approximately 50°C for about half an hour. You can also freeze seeds to kill off insects that may live inside the seed casings.

Drying

Drying the seeds is critical. Keep seeds at a temperature below 35°C and maintain good airflow to ensure that the seeds will thoroughly dry out within a couple of days.

Storage

Pack the seeds on a dry day and make sure the air stays dry, as moisture encourages growth and will rot the seed. Keep the seeds in airtight jars and make sure to label them all. At this stage of the process you'd hate to forget what seeds you have stored! A good rule of thumb for seed storage — the larger the seed, the longer they will keep. Store in a cool, dry place.

HOW TO
Save tomato seeds

Being a tad obsessed with tomatoes, we are stout advocates of saving our tomato seeds. They're our number one vegetable, and we would be lost if we boarded a boat that capsized and our seeds were not secured inside a jar, inside a jar, inside a jar.

For this extremely important activity you will require:

> your chosen tomatoes
> small jar with airtight lid
> sieve
> water
> kitchen plate or chopping board
> adhesive label
> pen

Gather a selection of tomatoes from your best performing tomato plants this season. Consider their yield, taste, colour, hardiness, resistance to pests and, inexplicably, the process of falling in love with a plant for apparently no reason.

2 Keeping each variety separate, pulp the tomatoes and transfer to your jar.

Add water and leave to sit overnight. This helps to dislodge the seed from the jelly-like pulp.

4 Empty the contents of the jar into a sieve, place it under running water to remove the last of the pulp.

Place the clean seeds on a plate and allow to dry.

Once the seeds are dry (after a few days), gently scrape any remaining pulp off the surface of the seeds and transfer the seeds to an airtight jar.

Label with the variety and the date.

Store in a dry, cool place.

EVERYONE SHOULD COMPOST

If you are not composting, you are without doubt contributing a lot of unnecessary waste to landfill. That waste sits in large, smouldering piles, creating and then emitting carbon dioxide, which forcefully argues with the atmosphere and aggressively wins. But your waste could be turned into a useful organic matter that is excellent for your vegetable garden and also saves our atmosphere great headaches.

Nearly all of our household waste is either recyclable or compostable. Since we began composting with vigour, our general waste bins have been living easy lives. Our compost piles, on the other hand, have become work horses.

Composting has been occurring naturally since plant life began. Leaves and plants constantly fall to the forest floor where they decompose back into the soil structure, contributing to new life. The living plants take up the nutrients offered by the dead and decaying old life, and this process repeats itself in a continuous cycle.

In our line of work we come across a number of compost units, all in varying states of health. More often than not, compost piles lie neglected and dried up. Empty them out and they tell the story of a household that more than likely had one great garden clean up, including that of the vagrant litter lying around, and then stuffed it all into their brand new compost unit. They then played the waiting game. The good workforce that are responsible for the decomposition process don't operate in these conditions and they played their waiting game too. And so nothing else happened.

We also encounter saturated and slimy units, mainly through over-enthusiasm rather than neglect. Empty it and you generally find a stinky pile of raw food scraps. In this case, an anaerobic process is occurring, where the lack of oxygen in the scraps suffocates the good workers and prevents them from completing their responsibilities, while troublemakers take up the slack, creating carbon dioxide.

You may be surprised to hear that far more often we encounter a compost pile that is in good working order. So, you're asking yourself, how are these people and their compost different?

Like so many things in the garden, making good compost is about finding a balance and following some basic rules. It's about getting into a routine and making that routine a habit. It isn't hard, and it shouldn't seem daunting. First, it is important to understand what composting is and how it works.

How composting works

Composting is the transformation of plant and food matter through decomposition into a dark, rich, crumbly material — compost. The process gets under way once your compost pile creates the ideal conditions for hard and honest workers — that is, microbes (tiny soil micro-organisms) and often worms and insects as well, to break the ingredients down into a substance that is laden with nutrition for your plants.

Creating these ideal conditions is where a lot of people start making mistakes. The compost pile needs the right mix of natural waste, of both the green (wet) and brown (dry) waste forms. More simply, your pile needs to contain moisture, food and air to work, and these two types of waste provide those elements.

> **Green wastes** Grass clippings, green weeds and garden waste, fruit and vegetable wastes, coffee grounds, eggshells, tea bags.

> **Brown wastes** Dry leaves, straw, hay, dead weeds and garden waste, wood chips, sawdust.

> **Not compostable** Meat scraps, bones, human waste, pet waste, chemically treated wood products, noxious and/or invasive weeds, diseased plants.

Generally, the greater the volume of waste, the greater the ability of the pile to create the ideal feeding and breeding conditions for the microbes. As long as food, moisture and air are available, the microbes are more than willing to continue building their highly efficient food-processing community. When food is lacking, they search elsewhere; when moisture is lacking, they run for cover; when air is lacking, they are overrun by troublemakers with atrocious eating habits.

We recommend you keep a lidded bin in your kitchen specifically for collecting your green wastes. Otherwise discarding such wastes with the rest of your garbage may seem more appealing than making constant trips to the compost bin.

Compost lasagne

You can create the ideal conditions for honest and hard-working microbes by creating a compost lasagne of alternating green and brown layers: 2 parts brown to 1 part green. As you combine the two types of waste, the contents heat up, encouraging the microbes and other useful organisms to come in and feed 'n' breed.

Green wastes are generally high in moisture content and contain high amounts of nitrogen that provides protein for the microbes. Brown wastes consist of mainly dead plant waste that provides air and a source of energy for the microbes. To ensure there is sufficient moisture, briefly water your brown waste before adding it to your pile.

If you notice your 'lasagne' becoming smelly because of excessive moisture, you will need to add more brown waste and manually turn the contents over to dry and air out the pile, stopping the anaerobic process. If your pile looks dry and lifeless, it will require more food and moisture as well as turning over.

Composting temperature

You will need at least one cubic metre of ingredients to create the ideal temperature of 60°C at the pile's centre; this is the temperature at which absolute compost is made and the hardiest of materials are broken down. You won't find this temperature on the outside of the heap — that's why you need to turn the compost and incorporate all the materials to reach the central core temperature. Get into the routine of turning over your pile at least once a fortnight; once a week is even better.

If your compost pile doesn't reach 60°C, some plant matter will survive the process and inevitably be reintegrated back into your garden as weeds. With luck, you might find a tomato plant sprouting from your compost bins, but if a tomato seed can germinate, then the seed of a noxious weed is also just as likely to emerge!

Composting bays

Ideally, we prefer to use large, rotatable compost bays, each one a cubic metre in volume or greater, to create the perfect compost. Unfortunately, most homes don't have enough space, and most gardeners don't have the energy and time required to constantly maintain them. Most of us will therefore opt for a domestic-sized unit that strikes a balance between efficient composting and ease of use.

If you don't have space for a compost bin, try trench composting, which involves digging your kitchen scraps directly into your patch at least 20 cm deep. In the earth they will decompose and compost, releasing nutrients for your plants. A Bokashi unit, which we discuss opposite, is another space-saving alternative.

There are two main styles of compost bin on the market — rotating and standalone. The ones with rotating wheels are easiest to use, but their size constraints probably make them the most inefficient. The standalone units are probably the most common and recognisable, and they work best, as they are generally larger and stand on open ground, allowing worms to engage in the process. However, these do require the most dedication.

A sad but true fact is that good composting is inevitably a labour-intensive activity. The amount of effort a composting unit requires is more often than not positively correlated to the unit's effectiveness. Therefore, finding a system that suits your level of dedication, then using it to the best of its ability, will result in great benefits for your vegetable garden and help to reduce unnecessary landfill.

Your compost is ready when it takes on the appearance of soil rather than a combination of your food and garden wastes. Integrate it through the soil at a depth of 20–30 cm prior to planting or, alternatively, sprinkle it around the base of your plants and water in.

Bokashi

A Japanese word meaning 'fermented organic matter', bokashi is a type of composting that relies on an anaerobic process to decompose and create organic matter. Bokashi units are compact and airtight, containing the wastes that essentially ferment while interacting with a solution made up of wheat bran, water, molasses and microbes. The bokashi process does not release any methane or carbon dioxide.

Bokashi units are suitable for small home-owners and apartment dwellers who do not produce enough waste or the right type of waste for composting.

The waste in the bokashi takes about a fortnight to ferment properly; a sweet vinegary smell or cotton-like fungi growing inside the unit is evidence of good fermentation. Use it in your veggie patches by digging it into the soil, then covering it. A lot of bokaski owners prefer to use only the juice that is extracted from the unit via a release valve. This juice is diluted with water and then used as a complete plant tonic.

Make a compost aerator

One way to prevent aeration problems in your compost pile is to use a compost aerator that creates an air pocket, allowing your waste to breathe. The aerator allows adequate airflow through your compost pile so it doesn't turn stinky. While the aerator will reduce the ability of the pile to heat up to that all-important 60°C, losing a bit of heat is more than compensated by significantly reducing the amount of work involved in composting.

Ideally, a compost aerator should be fixed to the unit before you start filling it with waste. However, the aerator can also be the solution for wet, stinky piles that may seem unredeemable.

Here's what you will need:

> length of PVC pipe (between 60 and 100 mm in diameter)

> measuring tape

> hacksaw

> drill

> 10-mm drill bit

> thin stake

> vice

> mallet or hammer

> small amount of brown waste, such as pea straw

Measure the height of your compost bin or pile.

Secure the PVC pipe in your vice and, using a hacksaw, cut to the height of your compost bin or pile.

Using a 10 mm drill bit, drill holes at regular and frequent intervals up the PVC pipe, all the way from the bottom to the top.

Here's the tricky part — make a hole in the centre of your compost heap. Start with something thin, such as a garden stake, driving it with a hammer or mallet through the centre to the bottom and moving in a circular motion. As the hole gets bigger, you can move onto thicker materials until the hole is big enough.

5 Drive the pipe into the centre of the compost heap.

6 Add some brown material such as pea straw to the top of the pile to soak up the moisture attempting to evaporate through the mix.

Stench alleviated!

THE
BENEFITS
OF WORMS

There is nothing more widely acclaimed for its ability to poo than the worm. There were occasions when a toddler nephew of ours, Sam, thought his poo was the greatest show on earth, but even Sam's poo doesn't stack up to that of the worm. Worm poo is number one.

Worm poo, or worm castings to put it nicely, is the result of worms ingesting your garden and food waste, then releasing them as castings (let's face it, as poo), which are up to ten times more fertile.

Worm farming, or 'vermicomposting', is a process not dissimilar to that of composting, but with an even more valuable outcome for your vegetable garden. The castings produced by worms are a nutrient-rich organic fertiliser and important soil conditioner. They act as a conduit, helping to convert and pass on the nutrients in your soil to your plants. Your soil may contain all the necessary elements for growing great crops, but if your plants are unable to convert and feed, they can be rendered highly ineffective.

Just watching the worms devour their food is intriguing. How things so disgusting to touch can create something so beautiful to touch is thoroughly amazing. For those who have never touched worm poo, please do so immediately. You may first need to cure a small case of coprophobia, but running your hand through a small amount of worm poo may be a step in the right direction. It is a rich, friable substance, dark chocolate in colour and completely odourless. What truffles are to the cook, worm poo is to the veggie gardener.

Worms

Special breeds of worm are necessary for worm farming, namely tiger worms and/or red worms, which are commonly available at nurseries. While the earthworm is also capable of producing castings, it does not have the same voracious appetite as its colleagues, so it's less effective.

It is quite staggering just how much food a tiger or red worm can eat and digest — up to half its body weight in a single day! Providing the right conditions for the worms will improve their eating ability and the amount of food they can process, plus multiply their numbers, thus providing you with more mouths to feed — in this case a great thing.

A worm farm can be as small or as large as you desire, making it suitable for smaller households and even apartments that don't have the space or waste necessary for composting. Not only will your farm create the worm castings, it will also produce a subsidiary liquid product known as worm wee. When diluted, this can be used as a liquid fertiliser on your vegetables.

Worm fundamentals

Worms don't like extreme heat or cold, so the first rule is to choose a well-insulated material from which to construct your farm, or a protected spot out of the sun. Your farm will need at least three levels.

1 The worm farm will need to be elevated in order for the worm wee to be drained and collected. You can simply use another polystyrene box for this.

2 The second box will catch the worm wee to be used as liquid fertiliser. It will require an outlet point from which to drain the wee.

3 The second level is the worms' living space. It will have holes in the bottom, and contain 10–15 cm of bedding material to give them a grand homecoming. The bedding should primarily be made out of compost and wetted peat, with shredded paper and finely pulverised straw incorporated, watered in to make it moist. Add 1000–2000 worms, then place a thick layer of wetted newspaper or hessian over the bedding to keep it moist and dark (just the way worms like it). Allow them to settle in for a few days before setting them to work. You can then start adding kitchen scraps and waste for them to feed on, and they will produce their castings.

4 The third level will be identical to the second, again with holes in the bottom, but this time with a lid on top. Once the food on the second level becomes exhausted and all that remains is castings, the worms will travel to the third level to feed and repeat the process. First you will need to create their new living space (as described in Step 3 above) to encourage them to do so. At this point the second level should be empty of worms and full of worm castings, which you should use sparingly throughout your garden.

Another fundamental is knowing what type of waste your worms will love and what they really won't fancy.

> **Love** Coffee grounds, fruit and vegetable scraps, tea bags, leaves, paper and cardboard, eggshells.

> **Don't fancy** Large quantities of animal manures, onion family, citrus family, dairy products, meat.

Food preparation

Worms will eat almost anything you throw at them and will manage to break it down to some degree, but for domestic purposes the efficiency of a worm farm can be improved if you remember there is no point throwing in ingredients whole. Remember: worms don't have a knife and fork, nor do they have hands, so put yourself in the worm's position and imagine being fed giant pieces of food with only your mouth to use. It's a good idea to shred whatever waste you have as finely as possible before adding it to the worm farm. This will greatly speed up the process.

When to feed

Determine when your worms are hungry and when they are full. Dried mixes or mixes full of castings signal that the worms are hungry and require food. Wet mixes that are starting to smell indicate that the worms cannot eat as fast as you are feeding them, and they probably need some breathing space. This is quite common in households that are overexcited about their new worm friends, so be sure to check on them from time to time.

The happier your worms are, the faster they will multiply and then the faster they will break down your wastes. Worms lay one egg a week, so their numbers will multiply pretty quickly if the conditions are right. Quite often your initial worm farm will become overpopulated, and at that point you'll need to consider investing in another farm, or a larger one.

Make a worm farm

You can use a number of different materials to make a worm farm. What you need is a material with insulation and longevity, which is why we use old freezer insulation to create our boxes. While this may be a little hard for you to source, polystyrene boxes are easy to find and very effective. They are also very simple to piece together, and by using them as a worm farm, you save them from becoming premature landfill.

A sad practice of green grocers is the use of polystyrene to transport food. However, this is where you can go to source the materials you require for constructing your worm farm.

We are looking for boxes with a depth of 20 cm or more and of a suitable size for the space you have available. Ask your fruiterer nicely, or tell him or her you love them. If you can't source a lid, thick cardboard will do.

For this activity you'll need:

> 4 polystyrene boxes (one with lid)

> pencil or biro (or a drill)

> small bowl for collecting worm wee

> bedding material – wetted peat block, newspaper and some compost

> newspaper (not one you haven't read yet) or hessian bag

> 20-litre bag of compost

> 1000–2000 red or tiger worms

wee receptacle

Use a pencil, biro or drill to poke a hole in one end of box number 2. This will sit on top of box number 1, slightly staggered (see pic on previous page), to allow the worm wee to drain into your collection vessel, placed directly underneath the hole.

Use a biro, pencil or drill to poke holes through the base of boxes 3 and 4. Go crazy here — the worms like lots of room to move and these will be the entry points.

Place box number 3 on top of box number 2 and bring in 10–15 cm of bedding material.

Add the worms to box number 3!!!!! Cover with wetted newspaper hessian bag and let the guys settle in.

5 After some days, start putting in your kitchen waste to feed the hungry worms, always covering it with the damp newspaper or hessian bag and replacing the lid.

6 Once box number 3 is full of castings and you cannot fit in any more waste, repeat the bedding procedure in box number 4 and place it on top of box number 3. Top with the lid.

The worms will move from box number 3 to box number 4, leaving you with their poo in box number 3 and wee draining into your bowl!

8 Once the worms have vacated box number 3, rotate the boxes once again (as per step 3), use their castings on the garden and watch in wonder.

GROWING FRUIT TREES

'I have this recurring dream in which I awake to find a beautiful woman stewing fruits in my kitchen. She's not naked, in fact she's clothed in a vintage checked cotton dress, with a checked cotton apron (slightly clashing) and she's stewing and bottling red-fleshed plums. I have left my bed to join her, led by the humid, scented air to the coloured pots boiling on the stove. My eyes are tired from oversleeping, but as I join in bottling the fruits, I glimpse out the kitchen window to my backyard and a mini fruit orchard, in full autumn fruit. 'Where's my work truck? What happened to my shed?' I look at her sternly, "It's plums this time, isn't it...?"

A mini fruit orchard isn't completely unrealistic where I live, but to have one I'd have to forfeit my shed and secure parking spot. Living in the city unfortunately dictates that practicality takes precedence over my concoctions of idyllic living, where fruit trees and perpetual home-cooking play major roles. In truth I want to be like Hugh Fearnley-Whittingstall in his River Cottage, where everything is as perfect as a well edited TV show. But is my life really that far off that fantasy? I do have fruit trees in my backyard, I do stew and pickle fruits, albeit without a beautiful woman in a vintage dress, and I am writing a book that I hope will be very well edited! Perhaps I'm closer to my dream than I realise.

When I moved to my home in Thornbury, Melbourne, I inherited a style of living that had been fashioned by the Europeans who established my community. The idea that their gardens should function around fruit trees and vegetable plots was second nature to them, and while property prices and age have thinned out the current European community, their legacy remains and my suburb is littered with old, evolved, prolific fruit trees.

Most autumn days I will drive my ute down my laneway over kilos and kilos of ripe, fallen fruit. Some days I will stop below the branch of either an apple or plum or fig or apricot tree and eat fruit until I reach the fine balance between being satisfied and sick. I've considered opening up the laneway to our clients for a day of free-for-all fruit picking, but either selfishness or laziness gets in the way.

My laneway is a great example of the potential of fruit trees and what they can offer. Most of them go largely unmaintained and neglected, but each year, with little fuss, they produce their fruit. They also help to create a thriving and diverse mini-ecosystem that attracts birds and insects to pollinate plants and control pests. This in turn contributes to the success of my vegetable garden, naturally becoming part of that chain.' –MP

If you are not fortunate enough to have established fruit trees in your garden or neighbourhood, it is surely worth considering growing them. The amount of space required is much less than you might think, and fruit trees can be incorporated into the dynamic of your garden with little fuss. So whether you have a small plot of land, courtyard or balcony, there will surely be enough room to accommodate at least one fruit tree.

Selecting your plants

The first thing you will need to consider is what fruit you like eating. Just as there's no point in planting veggies you don't like and simply don't eat, you wouldn't choose to plant fruit trees if you don't like eating their fruit. The next step, and the more decisive factor, is to determine what fruit trees are suited to your climatic conditions. One way of figuring this out is to take a stroll through your neighbourhood and notice which fruit trees are doing well. I often come across plums thriving in my area, so I have planted some varieties of these. If you can't find mango trees, there is probably a good reason.

Determine what sort of tree is likely to fit in your space. Planting dwarf rootstock, a grafted tree that self-pollinates or two cross-pollinating trees in the same hole are all ways of maximising your available space. Another space-saving technique is to espalier fruit trees, which means pruning the tree to create a flat plane of growing branches, making them ideal for growing up against walls or in thin rows. Not all trees can be espaliered, so make sure your variety is suitable.

Planting fruit trees in pots is also worth pursuing when space restraints allow no other option. Choose varieties that will suit this form of growing, such as dwarf rootstock, and provide the largest pot you can afford to improve your chances of success. Potted trees will require more upkeep than those in the ground, as they tend to use up water and nutrients at a faster rate, so keep a critical eye on their progress.

During winter, look in nurseries for bare-rooted fruit trees (those without soil around their roots). This is the ideal time to plant, as the trees will be dormant. And don't be alarmed when the nursery prunes back the branches when you purchase them; this simply helps the tree survive the transplant, and the branches will grow back with vigour!

Soil preparation

Fruit trees like a regular supply of water and also a free-draining soil. The more regular the supply of water, the better fruit your tree will produce, so consider investing in irrigation for your trees — drip irrigation is most effective (see page 25). If your soil is heavily clay-based,
incorporate organic matter and potentially gypsum or lime to break it up. People fall into the trap of planting fruit trees directly into clay and then wonder why they fail to grow. Clay badly restricts root growth, causing them to grow back onto themselves and stunting the growth of the tree. Clay can also hold water and pool, causing the roots to become waterlogged and they can rot.

If you are faced with clay, ensure you dig a larger than necessary planting hole and backfill with good topsoil and compost. Sandy soil will also need to be improved to hold the moisture and nutrients that a fruit tree requires. Again, add organic matter. Soil preparation is just as important for fruit trees as it is for vegetables.

Pollination

As mentioned previously, you must consider the issue of pollination, the process whereby the flowers become fertilised and then the fruit sets. Without pollination there is no fruit, and not all fruit trees pollinate in the same fashion. Some trees are self-pollinating (all citrus, for example), whereas others require cross-pollination from a tree nearby.

First ask your neighbours if they have suitable breeding partners for your new fruit trees. Another tree of the same species (and opposite sex of course!) will need to be within 30–50 m for it to be effectively pollinated, so doorknocking more than a couple of houses to find out is just flirting and nothing more. If you come up empty you'll need to plant a cross-pollinating tree as well, and these should both be planted in the same hole. Alternatively, plant a grafted tree – that is a single tree that has both varieties grafted on to the root stock. This will cross-pollinate.

Chilling hours

Fruit and nut varieties from cooler climates need a certain number of 'chilling hours' per year in order to properly set fruit. A chilling hour refers to an hour spent at a temperature of 7°C or less. For example, most species of apple trees will require between 500 and 600 chill hours each year in order to produce fruit. For this reason, check your temperature averages to ensure you are not planting a tree in vain.

HOW TO
Plant a fruit tree

To plant you'll need:

> your fruit tree!
> spade or shovel
> 40-litre bag of compost
> small amount of slow-release
  organic fertiliser
> 2 × 1.5 m wooden stakes
> soft twine
> pea straw

1 Choose a well-drained, sunny spot that is large enough to accommodate the mature tree.

2 Dig a hole slightly shallower than the height of the root ball you are planting, clearing any surrounding grass and roots that will compete for water.

3 Viden the hole to about twice the width of the root ball — the roots f fruit trees travel wide but close to the surface in search of water nd to stabilise themselves.

4 Wet the hole with 10 litres of water to moisten the surrounding soil thoroughly.

Position your fruit tree in the hole so that the shape of the existing canopy suits how you would like it to grow out when it matures. Backfill with topsoil mixed with extra compost, creating a well that directs the water to its roots and packing down as you do so. Water thoroughly.

Sprinkle with some slow-release organic fertiliser.

Drive in two stakes, about 30 cm on either side of the trunk, and use soft twine to tie the trunk to the stakes and hold the tree perfectly upright.

Mulch thoroughly with pea straw, keeping the mulch away from the trunk of the tree.

Pruning

Once your fruit trees are growing, it is worthwhile pruning them regularly. Like all plants, trees grow upwards in search of sunlight; however, taking your fruit to the sky makes fruit harvesting a mostly dangerous pastime. The idea is to keep the productive branches within reach for harvest, so you want to encourage the plant to grow out rather than up. Trees also prefer good air circulation to reduce their susceptibility to pests and diseases, so creating an air pocket through the centre by removing overcrowding branches there will help. Ideally, you should aim to create the shape of a vase as you prune.

Also keep on top of any suckers growing from the root ball or below the graft of the plant. These useless and annoying growths divert the growing energy from the main stem.

When pruning any tree, particularly those you love with all your heart, use clean and sharp tools to prevent splitting and hacking away at limbs, not to mention passing on any disease or infection.

Evergreen fruit trees will require one main pruning each season, and this is best done in early Spring, after the last frost. With deciduous trees, it has long been held that you should prune them only once during the dormant winter months; however, the new school of thought teaches two smaller pruning efforts — one during winter when the plant is dormant and the second in summer/autumn, just after fruiting. The idea here is that the winter prune will create more vigorous new growth the following season (the new growth is where you get most of your fruit!), while a summer prune keeps the overall health and shape of the tree in check. Trees are susceptible to disease immediately after pruning, so feed them with a slow-release organic fertiliser and water well to give them a boost.

Fruit trees should not be perceived as 'too much hard work'. They are great contributors to any productive garden, and from the trees come summer and autumn days in the kitchen stewing the fruits, perhaps with a beautiful woman dressed in checked cotton, who knows? So next time you're considering planting another Silver Birch or Manchurian pear, think about how much more pleasure the right fruit tree could provide.

A–Z OF
EDIBLE PLANTS

APPLE

Rule Number 1 for growing fruit trees at home — keep the tree size and shape manageable for harvesting. Sometimes this is easier said than done.

For the first 30 years of its life, the giant apple tree next door may have been a harvesting delight. Not the case in more recent times. When one of us moved into a new neighbourhood, Rita, the lovely next-door neighbour, saw a couple of 'young, strong, fit men' as an opportunity to restore her apple tree. Her approach was ingenious and we were immediately on her side; it was the first time since cleaning a relative's gutters that any of us had been called young, strong, fit and a man in one sentence.

The cut-back effort took three concerted attempts, and despite our ability to pack down green waste, it required two trips to the tip. The tree is now closer to 4 m than 6 m in height, the inner section is breathing again and overall the tree has a more defined shape. The fruit is still a little sour, but we hope to get a better developed, sweeter harvest in future. The restoration process will take some time — more than a year or two to reverse 20 years of neglect — but there is the feeling it will prove more than worthwhile. It has certainly proved that, at 76 years of age, Rita still has it.

Botanical name
Malus domestica

Family
Rosaceae (Rose family)

Origin
Asia and the Middle East

Little Veggie Patch favourite
Royal Gala

Space needs
Can be grown in larger pots, but prefers being in-ground

Companion plants
Garlic, onion, chives, nasturtium

How to grow
Plant as bare-rooted stock in autumn through to winter, otherwise transplant bagged or potted varieties in spring.

When to plant
> Zone 1: May–November
> Zone 2: May–November
> Zone 3: May–November
> Zone 4: June–October

Soil preparation
Prepare the soil so that it is free-draining and integrated with compost and well-rotted animal manure.

pH level
6.0–7.5

Position
Full sun, preferably a sheltered spot. Can be espaliered against a shed or fence.

Spacing
3–10 m, depending on the variety

Problems
Aphids, powdery mildew

Considered one of the first trees to be cultivated, apples are deciduous, and most varieties require a cross-pollinator within 30–50 m of each other in order to cross-pollinate. They will produce decent fruit after 3–6 years. There are now more than 7500 known cultivars, and for the home grower there are hybrid varieties and dwarf rootstocks that help to conserve space. You should be aware that fruiting of rootstockwill take much longer, up to 9–12 years. Apples will typically need between 500 and 600chilling hours each year to set fruit (see page 55).

Dig a hole twice the width of the root ball, but a little shallower than the root ball's height, thereby allowing you to mound the soil and create a well for drainage purposes. Before positioning the plant, water the hole with approximately 10 litres to allow the moisture to penetrate the area around the hole.

Position your tree, then backfill with soil, firming down and watering in as you do so. Create a mound and furrow to help drain the water and direct it down to the root system.

Drive in two stakes, about 30 cm on either side of the trunk, and use soft twine to tie the trunk to the stakes and hold the plant perfectly upright.

Feeding and mulching

During the planting process, apply a handful of slow-release organic fertiliser, then water in thoroughly. Mulch around the base of the tree with pea straw or lucerne hay, to a depth of 5–10 cm, keeping the mulch away from the plant's stem. Once a year, before fruiting, feed your apple tree with a heavy nitrogen-based fertiliser.

Watering

Water in well, 2–3 times a week for the first month. Keep on top of any encroaching weeds or grass. Thereafter, in the absence of rainfall, water once a week for the first year.

Pruning

With all fruit trees, pruning is very important, but especially so with apple trees, as they will eventually have to bear heavy loads of fruit. If you are espaliering your tree, define 3–4 horizontal limbs, then use soft twine to attach them securely to a trellis or fence. Keep other growth in check so the tree can concentrate its growing efforts on those branches.

If you are shaping a standalone tree, define 3–4 main limbs and create a shape that will result in an easy harvest, good airflow and the tree being able to hold the weight of the fruit. (Good airflow will help keep fungal diseases and other pests at bay.) One option is to angle the main fruiting limbs at 45–60 degrees from the main trunk — at this angle they will be best able to hold the fruiting weight and less likely to split under duress. The shape you create has to fulfill two criteria — ease of picking and the ability to hold fruit. If the branches are vertical, they will hold the fruit but be hard to pick; if they are horizontal, they will be easier to pick, but may split under their heavy load.

Harvesting

When your apples are a decent size and regularly falling to the ground, it is time to harvest, although the best test is a smell-and-taste trial. Not all the apples will be ready at once, so choose from clusters that you have deduced are ripe. Hand-pick individual apples by twisting the apple with one hand while you brace the branch with the other, or prune off clusters. Be careful when handling the fruit, as it will bruise easily.

Remove any apples that fall to the ground before ripening so they won't attract pests and diseases.

ARTICHOKE (globe)

Upon first impression a globe artichoke can seem like a lot of growing hoo-ha for marginal edible reward. This is particularly true during the first season, when developed hearts are uncommon, plant growth is prolific and you start branding your artichoke fat and useless. But this all changes the following season, when your useless plant turns useful, producing a number of edible hearts; it will go on increasing its yield for up to 5 years.

An artichoke heart is a fierce culinary weapon that will impress even the most critical of your foodie friends. The plant itself is just as impressive, with its glossy silver leaves branching out to form a small bush when mature. Its perennial growth will buoy your spirits when the veggie patch is empty between seasons, and it can also be used to form an herbaceous border, attracting pollinating insects to your garden.

Be patient with artichokes and you will be rewarded.

Botanical name
Cynara scolymus

Family
Asteraceae (Daisy family)

Origin
Mediterranean and
Central Asia

Little Veggie Patch favourite
Purple Headed

Space needs
Best grown in an in-ground
veggie patch

Companion plant
Asparagus

How to grow
Sow seeds directly into your
patch

When to plant
>Zone 1: September–November
>Zone 2: August–November
>Zone 3: August–November
>Zone 4: April–July

Soil preparation
Artichokes grow well in sandy,
free-draining soil. Add compost
and pelletised chicken manure
prior to planting.

pH level
6.0–6.8

Position
Full sun

Spacing
1.5 m

Problems
Aphids, ants

ARTICHOKE (globe)

Sow seed at a depth that is 2–3 times the diameter of the seed, then backfill with soil, lightly firm down and water thoroughly. When your plants start to develop hearts, usually from the second season onwards, you may need to provide the plant with some support. Replace plants that are older than 5 years.

Artichokes send out suckers that can be removed and transplanted elsewhere, giving you the opportunity to develop new plants as the older ones mature. Carefully pull out the suckers, with their roots intact, and replant them in a suitable space.

Feeding and mulching

Feed your artichokes with a low-nitrogen organic fertiliser twice a year and you will be rewarded with a higher yield. To keep the soil temperature constant and lock in moisture, mulch with 3–5 cm of lucerne hay or pea straw.

Watering

While the plant is establishing, water regularly, 2–3 times a week. Once a week will suffice for mature plants.

Harvesting

Start harvesting when the plant produces buds or hearts. Cut each one off at the stem, about 5 cm below the heart, when they are about the size of a fist and before they start opening.

Nonna's Kitchen

Stuffed artichokes

4 artichoke hearts
200 g breadcrumbs
handful flat-leaf parsley, chopped
1 garlic clove, finely chopped
50 g parmesan, finely grated
1 pork sausage (optional)
salt and freshly ground black pepper
olive oil

> Harvest the artichoke hearts before they go to flower, cutting the stems at a length of 3–5 cm from the head.

> Remove the hard outer leaves of the artichoke heart until you get to the softer tender growth. Cut off the stem lengths at the base of the flower, peel the tough skin from the stems and put the stems aside.

> To make the stuffing, mix the breadcrumbs with the parsley, garlic, parmesan and Nonna's homemade sausage (if using). Mix well and season with salt and pepper.

> Using a knife, cut across the top of each artichoke to leave you with a flat surface. Now get stuffing. Work the stuffing in between the leaves and press down firmly until there is an even coating across the top of the artichoke hearts.

> Heat up a pan with a good lug of oil in it, and gently fry the tops of the artichoke hearts for a few minutes until golden brown.

> Transfer the hearts and peeled stems to a pot, cover with salted water and gently bring to a simmer. Cover (with a lid that has an air valve) and cook until the water has almost evaporated. This should take roughly an hour.

> Devour.

Serves 4

ASPARAGUS

This ferny-looking perennial plant produces tender green crowns 2–3 seasons after planting, but it is a worthwhile investment, as your plants will continue to produce for more than 20 years.

Asparagus plants can be either female or male, with the male plants producing fatter crowns, so it is a good idea to check on the varieties before planting. It's a matter of personal taste, and we tend to go for the slimmer female varieties. But each to their own…

Foodies attest that better quality asparagus comes from cooler regions. If you live in a warmer area, it is important to 'catch' and harvest the crowns when they are at their optimum, as the quality quickly deteriorates once they are allowed to grow past 25 cm.

To grow white asparagus, known as 'white gold', starve the crowns of sunlight by growing them under a thick layer of mulch and cutting the stems before they reach the surface.

Botanical name
Asparagus officinalis

Family
Liliaceae (Lily family)

Origin
Europe, Asia and North America

Little Veggie Patch favourite
Mary Washington

Space needs
Best grown in an in-ground veggie patch

Companion plants
Tomato, artichoke

How to grow
Sow seeds or plant crowns

When to plant
>Zone 1: September–November
>Zone 2: September–January
>Zone 3: August–November
>Zone 4: February–November

Soil preparation
Dig plenty of well-rotted manure into the soil to a depth of 20 cm. Add fresh chook manure a fortnight before planting.

pH level
6.0–7.0

Position
Full sun to part shade

Spacing
30 cm

Problem
Crown rot

You can grow asparagus from seed, but for a quicker harvest, sow crowns directly. Dig a trench to a depth of 15–20 cm, plant the crowns, then cover with pure compost. Water in thoroughly.

Asparagus crowns take 2–3 years to mature. In the first couple of years, avoid the temptation to cut the crowns, otherwise the plant won't develop.

Feeding and mulching

Feed asparagus well in autumn, before its dormant period, with compost and well-rotted manure. Regularly fertilise with liquid seaweed extract to help develop the crowns for harvest. To lock in moisture and also to blanch the crowns, use a thick layer of lucerne hay — anywhere between 5 and 20 cm, depending on the size of the crowns and how much of the stem you want to blanch.

Watering

Asparagus can cope with damp conditions and will thrive with regular, deep watering. However, be careful not to overwater as the crowns develop, or they will become susceptible to rot.

Harvesting

Pick the crowns in spring and into summer, when they are at the optimum length of 20–25 cm, or for a sweeter, more distinct taste, pick them when they are smaller. Depending on the sex of the plant, the spears will be approximately 5–10 mm in diameter, with the female species producing skinnier crowns than the male. Either pull them out by hand or, to avoid damaging other crowns, use a knife to cut each stem a few centimetres below the surface.

Towards the end of the harvesting period, it is important to leave the last few crowns to develop into ferny growth and support the plant during the dormancy period. This will prolong the life of your plant and ensure it is productive over its life.

BEANS

Fabian says that if he were a vegetable he would be a bean. A 'Scarlet Runner' specifically. That would mean he'd have crimson-red flowers growing from his hair before fruiting and then long green pods to eat off his fingers. If there were a person for each variety of bean, we'd have a thriving city, full of diversity.

The Legume family (Fabaceae) is one of the largest, and one of its members, the bean, comes in all shapes and sizes, in bush and climbing forms. Their edible pods may be flat or rounded, long or short, and may contain as few as 4 seeds or up to 12. The flowers can be white, yellow, pink or mauve, while the seeds and pods come in such a variety of colours and patterns that, when displayed together, they look like edible pirate treasure.

Beans are a summer crop, full of nitrogen. When your plants are finished, dig them back into the patch as green manure. Climbing beans, as the name implies, are an excellent crop to grow vertically if you're short of space.

Botanical name
Phaseolus vulgaris

Family
Fabaceae (Legume family)

Origin
South America

Little Veggie Patch favourite
Scarlet Runner

Space needs
Suited to larger pots, but prefer an in-ground veggie patch

Companion plants
Corn, marigold

How to grow
Sow seed directly into the patch

When to plant
> Zone 1: October–December
> Zone 2: September–February
> Zone 3: August–April
> Zone 4: Any time

Soil preparation
Beans fix your soil with nitrogen, which they produce naturally, so a moderately fertile, free-draining soil is required. A week prior to planting, apply compost and an application of potash to your soil. Ensure the pH level is within the recommended range.

pH level
6.5–7.0

Position
Full sun, preferably in an area that allows them to be trained vertically, thereby conserving space. Plant where you expect to grow brassicas the following season.

Spacing
15–20 cm

Problems
Snails and slugs, rodents, magnesium deficiency

Sow seed directly into the patch at a depth 2–3 times the diameter of the seed, then backfill with soil. Soak thoroughly after sowing, then avoid watering before germination, as bean seed has a tendency to rot.

Make sure you provide climbing varieties with an extensive support structure, but set this up before planting to avoid damaging the seeds/seedlings in the process. Keep the plant supported by your trellis as it grows, otherwise you may have to deal with an out-of-control 'Jack and the Beanstalk' at ground level.

If vertical growing is not possible, growing bush varieties is your best option — these won't require staking.

Feeding and mulching

Avoid overfertilising with nitrogen, as this will encourage prolific leaf growth at the expense of flower and pod development. During the growing season, water with diluted Epsom salts a couple of times to supply magnesium. See the packet for proportion details. Plants will also need an application of potassium (use liquid potash) before flowering to help them set fruit.

Watering

Water the seedlings 2–3 times a week for the first month. Water twice a week when flowering, otherwise once a week for mature plants.

Harvesting

Pick pods when they are at a desirable size. To avoid pulling off other parts of the plant, brace the stem with one hand and pick the pod with the other as you harvest. Regularly picking pods will encourage further crop production, so don't leave pods to overdevelop on the plant.

BEETROOT

Beetroot is a versatile vegetable, and one we always like to have growing in our patch. You can grow beetroot for both its root and leaves, and if you get a hankering for making a strong dye, beetroot is one of the best. It can be grown in most climates at most times of the year, so if you stagger your planting, you can enjoy a harvest almost all year round.

We've been told that beetroot is a form of aphrodisiac, and while this claim remains largely unsubstantiated, slow-roasting beets alongside a good cut of lamb, with caramelised onion and balsamic syrup, is pleasurable enough.

Botanical name
Beta vulgaris

Family
Chenopodiaceae (Beet family)

Origin
Mediterranean

Little Veggie Patch favourite
Detroit Dark Red

Space needs
Suited to smaller pots

Companion plant
Onion

How to grow
Sow seed directly into the patch

When to plant
>Zone 1: September–April
>Zone 2: July–April
>Zone 3: Any time
>Zone 4: Any time

Soil preparation
Dig well-rotted cow manure and compost into free-draining soil a week before planting.

pH level
6.5–7.0

Position
Full sun to part shade

Spacing
7–15 cm

Problems
Snails and slugs, magnesium deficiency

Sow seed directly into the patch at a depth of 1 cm, then brush over with soil, gently firm down and water in. Prior to planting, soak the seeds in water overnight to help the seeds germinate. A fortnight after the seeds have germinated, thin out the seedlings to allow each plant adequate space in which to grow.

The roots have a tendency to pop out of the ground, so you may need to mound the soil.

Feeding and mulching

Beetroot requires a good level of phosphorus and potassium. Avoid applying too much nitrogen, as this will lead to excessive foliage growth at the expense of the edible root. A fortnight after the seeds have germinated, mulch with lucerne hay or pea straw to a depth of 3–5 cm.

Watering

Water 2–3 times a week for the first month, then manage your watering to keep the ground moisture consistent. One water per week after that will ensure well-formed, juicy beets. Excessive watering may rot the roots.

Harvesting

Beets will be ready to harvest when the root is 5–10 cm in diameter. If left for too long in the soil, it will become tough and fibrous. When harvesting, use a garden fork to carefully dislodge it.

If the soil is well-drained and protected from frosts, the beets can be stored in the ground over winter, although you may need to apply another layer of mulch if the initial application has largely decomposed.

If you want to use the foliage in salads, get into the habit of spreading your picking over a number of plants — over-picking a few individual plants will affect their ability to photosynthesise.

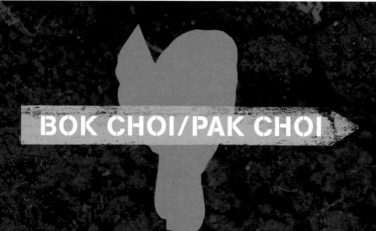

BOK CHOI/PAK CHOI

Bok choi or pak choi is the sort of vegetable we often find hard to resist as we walk through the market. Leafy, tender, Asian — it ticks all the boxes. Of course, we intend on putting it in Wednesday's stir-fry, most likely with oyster sauce, and it's a proud purchase at the checkout. Now stir-fry is not an unrealistic accomplishment — quite the opposite. It is dead easy. The problem is that the market is more than 100 head miles away from the kitchen, and somewhere along you way we get lost. Three weeks later that once proud, vibrant bok choi is often pulled from the base of the fridge's vegetable storage compartment, brown and soggy. At that point it's often a good opportunity to also pull out the gluey spring onions and almost completely decomposed silverbeet.

To avoid the bok choi episode becoming your groundhog day, it is a vegetable best grown at home.

Bok choi grows all year round, in most climates, and as they are shallow-rooted plants, they are perfectly suited to small pots and containers. For the novice gardener looking for a confidence boost, this is your vegetable.

Stagger your planting to give yourself the perpetual opportunity to cook it in a stir-fry with oyster sauce.

Botanical name
Brassica rapa, Chinensis Group

Family
Brassicaceae (Mustard family)

Origin
China

Little Veggie Patch favourite
Taisai

Space needs
Suited to smaller pots

Companion plants
Celery, onions

How to grow
Sow seed directly into the patch

When to plant
> Zone 1: September–April
> Zone 2: Any time
> Zone 3: Any time
> Zone 4: Any time

Soil preparation
Likes moist, fertile soil, requiring high levels of nitrogen for good leaf growth. Prepare your soil with plenty of organic matter prior to planting.

pH level
6.0–7.5

Position
Full sun to part shade

Spacing
20–30 cm

Problems
Mildew, slugs and snails

Sow seed directly into the patch at a depth of 0.5–1.0 cm, then backfill with soil and water in. Keep the soil moist until germination; however, even mature bok choi plants like some moisture in the soil at all times.

These prolific growers can be easily rotated for a continual harvest, so stagger your planting.

Feeding and mulching

This veggie is a big nitrogen feeder, and will appreciate weekly fertilising with liquid seaweed extract. To lock in moisture, keep the soil well-mulched with pea straw or lucerne hay to a depth of 3–5 cm.

Watering

Water 2–3 times a week until harvest, which should occur after 4–6 weeks.

Harvesting

You can harvest bok choi leaf by leaf or remove the entire plant when it is ready — cut the plant off with a knife a few centimetres above the ground and let the roots re-shoot new growth. You can repeat this process 2–3 times.

You may notice slugs and snails favouring some plants over others — leave these plants in as decoys/ sacrificial lambs.

WHERE DOES
OUR FOOD
COME FROM?

It is all too easy to forget where our food comes from. Seeing food in its living form is so rare these days that we have become increasingly detached from what we eat. Meat is red stuff wrapped in plastic, tomatoes are neatly stacked on a shelf and milk comes in either full cream or low-fat. Ask kids where baked beans come from and most ecstatically yell: 'A can!'

With most, if not all, of our food coming from the supermarket shelf, the connection between what we eat and where it comes from seems not so critical. Constant accessibility and reliability means that we can eat what we want, when we want it. But having our food needs so thoughtlessly and easily met has passed a reciprocal set of thoughtless and easy eating habits on to the next generation, creating an epidemic of Type II diabetes through childhood obesity. While society invests heavily in the treatment of diabetes, there is little being done to prevent and manage childhood obesity, a trigger of the disease.

There are various programs that have been implemented in Australian schools in recent years, aiming to develop a better relationship between kids and the food they eat — teaching them how to grow food in the garden and then prepare it in the kitchen. Allowing kids to establish a better relationship with food from an early age will encourage them to develop better eating habits that last a lifetime.

Growing beans in a bean can

Even before your kids start school, you can begin to educate them through fun projects that highlight the origins of their food.

Try growing vegetable seedlings in vegetable cans you commonly buy. But make sure you match the vegetable seedling to the type of tinned vegetable you are using. So if you're eating baked beans, grow some beans in that can. Any tinned vegetable will do, from corn and beetroot to peas and carrots.

For our example, we're using baked beans, so you will need:

> baked bean cans

> seed-raising mix

> bean seeds

> watering can

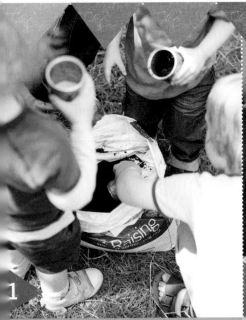

1

Open the cans carefully, paying particular attention to any sharp edges. Now empty out (that is, eat) in preparation. Wash the cans thoroughly.

2

Fill up your cans with seed-raising mix. As you do so, it's a good idea to press down and compact the soil slightly.

3

Sow 2 bean seeds at a depth of 2–3 cm in each can, then cover them with soil and firm down.

4

Water in thoroughly. The beans should not require further watering until germination, unless conditions are particularly dry.

5

Keep the cans out in the sunlight during the day and bring them in at night. Once the seeds have germinated and matured to a height of at least 15 cm, transplant them to the vegetable patch.

6

When the pods start forming, it's time to harvest the vegetables and eat them, comparing the taste with the canned variety!

BROAD BEANS

Broad beans have always occupied a large place in our hearts. Where would our tomato crop be without them? They are a most professional 'nitrogen fixer', and are routinely integrated into our soil at the end of the winter harvest, providing much needed aid to our nitrogen-greedy tomatoes. We learnt this technique from our grandparents, who would grow primarily tomatoes in spring and then broad beans in autumn. It's a relationship that worked for them and continues to work for us.

In case you're wondering where we stand with broad beans (are we just using broad beans to get to the tomato?), let's say our relationship is full and multilayered. As a stand-alone vegetable, it's one of our favourites and is used regularly in the kitchen. We also love the way it can almost support itself, clumsily defying physics. And, no less, we love the process of podding them — usually early and much to the dismay of any Italian grandparent.

Broad beans are easy to grow, and although they are more suited to cooler climates, and can be grown perennially in some, there are varieties, such as the Egyptian, that thrive in warmer climates too.

Botanical name
Vicia faba

Family
Fabaceae (Legume family)

Origin
Mediterranean and South-western Asia

Little Veggie Patch favourite
Crimson Red

Space needs
Suited to larger pots, but prefer an in-ground veggie patch

Companion plant
Potato

How to grow
Sow seed directly into the patch

When to plant
>Zone 1: February–September
>Zone 2: March–July
>Zone 3: March–June
>Zone 4: March–June

Soil preparation
Well-drained, relatively fertile soil. Like all beans, they will need higher amounts of phosphorus and potassium than nitrogen. A week prior to planting, apply compost and an application of potash to your soil.

pH level
6.5–7.5

Position
Full sun to part shade. Plant where you plan to grow your tomato crop next season.

Spacing
20–30 cm

Sow seed directly into the patch at a depth 2–3 times its diameter, then backfill with soil and gently firm down. Seeds will benefit from being soaked overnight prior to planting. Water in thoroughly after planting, then resist further watering until germination. Stagger your planting to ensure a continuous harvest as well as space for your first tomato plants in spring — the beans you planted first will make way for your first tomato seedings.

Once pods start to develop, you may need to support the plants, as they tend to fall over under the weight. Hilling up the soil around the plant stems as they grow will result in stronger plants and may reduce the need for staking.

To speed up development of the pods, pinch out the tips of the plant when flowers begin developing into little pods.

Feeding and mulching

Overfeeding the plant with nitrogen and manure can result in disease and fewer pods. Be sure your broad beans receive adequate levels of phosphorus and potassium, particularly when flowers and pods are forming. Apply a low-nitrogen fertiliser once during the growing season, and another application of potash before flowering. To maintain a consistent soil temperature, keep the soil well-mulched with pea straw or lucerne hay to a depth of 3–5 cm. Large changes in temperature can result in the flowers' failure to set pods.

Watering

After the seeds have germinated, water 2–3 times a week for the first month. Cut back to once a week as the plants mature, taking into account any rainfall. Their moisture requirement will increase while they are flowering and producing pods.

Harvesting

The pods are sweetest and tastiest when young, so pick to your taste requirements. Pick by hand, bracing the plant as you do so. Harvesting encourages other fruit to mature.

Once you are satisfied with the harvest, chop up and re-integrate the plant matter as a green manure.

BROCCOLI

First grown in Italy in the region of Calabria, broccoli made its way to the contemporary kitchen via the United States and Italian immigrants. As our grandparents' families came from areas surrounding Calabria, it seemed strange that they never grew broccoli. The truth was they were frightened by broccoli, and in fact by all members of the cabbage family, due to their propensity to attract pests, particularly the white cabbage moth. Their obsession with broad beans may also have hindered their acceptance of broccoli.

Since growing our own vegetables, we've had some great success with broccoli, and with relative ease too, which admittedly does not sit well with some of our grandparents.

We find that the key to good broccoli is definitely good preparation — preparation of your soil, and preparation against the pests that will try to strike.

Botanical name
Brassica oleraceae, Italica Group

Family
Brassicaceae (Mustard family)

Origin
Italy

Little Veggie Patch favourite
Romanesco

Space needs
Suited to larger pots, but prefer an in-ground veggie patch

Companion plants
Onion, dill, chamomile

How to grow
Propagate the seeds in individual seed cells or pots

When to plant
> Zone 1: October–March
> Zone 2: September–April
> Zone 3: February–May
> Zone 4: April–June

Soil preparation
Like all brassicas, broccoli have a high demand for nutrients, particularly nitrogen, so prepare your garden bed with green manure at the end of the previous season. Cut down your summer beans and turn them through the soil a couple of weeks before planting, then add well-rotted manure and compost.

pH level
6.0–7.0

Position
Sunny, well-drained spot. Rotate the spot in which you grow brassicas to avoid planting in the same place each year.

Spacing
45 cm

Problem
White cabbage moth

BROCCOLI

Sow seed into seed cells or pots, and at night keep indoors, away from any potential frost damage. Two to three weeks after germination, transplant to your veggie patch and water in with liquid seaweed fertiliser.

Apply fine netting over the young seedlings to prevent the white cabbage moth from laying its larvae on your broccoli. The seedlings are most susceptible when they are young and sweet.

Feeding and mulching

Broccoli are very hungry feeders. When stressed through lack of water and nutrients they tend to flower early, so feed them regularly. After transplanting, give them an application of liquid seaweed fertiliser once a fortnight, then mulch with pea straw or lucerne hay at a depth of 3–5 cm, keeping the mulch away from direct contact with the stem of the plant. Re-mulch mid-season.

Watering

Water 2–3 times a week when establishing, then cut back to once a week when the plants are mature. Adjust your watering for any rainfall.

Harvesting

Cut the initial large head with a knife at the head's base. After this first harvest, smaller side shoots, which are harvested as broccolini (smaller, less dense heads), will continually re-grow.

BRUSSELS SPROUTS

When this much-maligned vegetable is cooked properly, it is great to eat. If overcooked, it will emit a sulphurous odour that quite honestly smells like a damp fart. Do not overcook it.

Witnessing the growth of a brussels sprout plant is a slow form of entertainment. Its structure is highly original, almost contrived and unnatural, with sprouts growing out like edible balls holstered by batons, spiralling around the plant from top to bottom. If vegetable plants walked the catwalk, the brussel sprout would always turn heads.

The challenge in growing brussel sprouts is to produce dense sprouts, a stern test for the gardening enthusiast.

Botanical name
Brassica oleracea, Gemmifera Group

Family
Brassicaceae (Mustard family)

Origin
Western Europe

Little Veggie Patch favourite
Long Island Improved

Space needs
Suited to larger pots, but prefer an in-ground veggie patch

Companion plants
Onion, dill, chamomile

How to grow
Propagate the seeds in individual seed cells or pots

When to plant
>Zone 1: March–May
>Zone 2: March–June
>Zone 3: April–June
>Zone 4: April–July

Soil preparation
Prepare the space a fortnight before planting with a green manure, then integrate animal manure and compost into the mix.

pH level
6.5–7.5

Position
Sunny, well-drained position. Do not plant where brassicas grew in the previous season.

Spacing
60 cm

Problem
White cabbage moth

BRUSSELS SPROUTS

Sow seed into seed cells or pots at a depth of up to 2–3 times its diameter, cover with soil, then water in. Keep it indoors at night, away from any potential frost damage. A fortnight after germination, transplant the seedlings into your veggie patch, planting the roots deeply, so the soil comes a little up the stem. Mound the soil around the base of the plant to help establish a stronger root system.

To avoid damaging the roots at a later date when the plant is sprouting, position two stakes approximately 5–10 cm from the stem of the plant. To safeguard against attack by the white cabbage moth, place netting over the young seedlings.

Feeding and mulching

Give your plants a mid-season application of compost, but be careful not to over-apply nitrogen later in the growing process, as this will lead to puffy, loose sprouts. Picking off the yellowing leaves from the lower stems encourages the harvest to develop. To maintain even temperature and moisture, apply 3–5 cm of pea straw or lucerne hay.

Harvesting

Harvest the small sprouts that form off the plant's stem as soon as they are larger than a golf ball. It is best to cut them off, generally from the bottom to the top, as the more mature sprouts grow lower on the plant. They are best small and sweet, and harvesting them when they are younger will encourage the growth of other sprouts.

The outer leaves can also be harvested as a substitute for cabbage.

CABBAGE

Cabbage has been tagged 'the windy vegetable', perhaps even by itself, as that's the type of vegetable it is — honest to the core. This versatile vegetable is commonly eaten steamed, boiled, raw and/or pickled.

Like brussels sprouts, cabbage can omit a sulphurous odour when it is overcooked, but if you can get it right, cabbage is an excellent source of vitamin C, low in kilojoules, and it is said to be able to help heal ulcers and prevent cancer.

We love how cabbage can be used to turn soups into almost meaty meals, and how using our favoured variety, the red-headed 'Red Drumhead', can also add a touch of colour.

In Italian the word for cabbage, *cavolo*, can be used as a mild swear word, once again demonstrating its versatility.

As with all brassicas, the challenge is to achieve good head growth and keep pests at bay.

Botanical name
Brassica oleracea, Capitata Group

Family
Brassicaceae (Mustard family)

Origin
Mediterranean

Little Veggie Patch favourite
Red Drumhead

Space needs
Suited to larger pots, but prefer an in-ground veggie patch

Companion plants
Dill, onion, chamomile

How to grow
Propagate the seeds in individual seed cells or pots

When to plant
>Zone 1: August–May
>Zone 2: Any time
>Zone 3: Any time
>Zone 4: April–December

Soil preparation
Prepare your garden bed with green manure at the end of the previous season. Cut down your summer beans and turn them through the soil a couple of weeks before planting.

Add well-rotted manure and compost to increase the amount of organic matter in the soil.

pH level
6.5–7.5

Position
Sunny, well-drained spot in the patch. Avoid planting brassicas in the same place each year.

Spacing
60 cm

Problem
White cabbage moth

Sow seeds into individual cells or pots, cover with soil and water in. Keep indoors at night, away from any potential frost damage. A fortnight after germination, transplant the seedlings into your veggie patch, and water in with liquid seaweed fertiliser, covering them with fine netting to keep out the white cabbage moth.

As your cabbages grow, it is a good idea to mound soil around each stem to help the plants send out stabilising roots.

Feeding and mulching

Apply a liquid feed of seaweed extract every fortnight and compost mid-season. After planting, mulch thoroughly with a good layer of pea straw or lucerne hay to a depth of 3–5 cm. This may need to be repeated mid-season, depending on the level of decomposition.

Watering

Keep your cabbages well-watered to ensure a stress-free plant. Water your cabbage 2–3 times a week when the plants are adolescents, then cut back to one deep watering a week as they begin to mature.

Harvesting

Harvest the main head, cutting as far down the stem as possible. While secondary heads are possible, these are rarely worthwhile, so to avoid pests it is best to remove the whole plant after the initial harvest. The large outer leaves of the plant can be used to make rice and pork-mince cabbage rolls.

Nonna's Kitchen

Cabbage rolls

3 shallots, finely diced
2 garlic cloves, finely sliced
500 g pork mince
½ cup short grain rice, cooked
1 head of cabbage from the garden
1 brown onion, diced
2 x 750 ml bottles sugo (see page194 for recipe)
2 tablespoons olive oil
salt and freshly ground black pepper

> To prepare the filling, gently sauté the shallots and garlic for about 5 minutes until they are translucent. Add the pork mince and stir until it starts to brown. Add the cooked rice and mix well then take off the heat.

> Pick four outer leaves of the cabbage. Choose ones that are devoid of caterpillar attack, though one or two holes won't matter. Reserve the rest of cabbage, as you will need this later.

> Before you roll the leaves, blanch them in boiling water for a minute or two – this will make them more malleable. Cut out the thickest/toughest part of the leaf spine to help make rolling easier.

> Place a handful of filling in the centre of each leaf and roll up, tucking in the ends. Place rolls on a plate with the edge face down.

> Sauté the onion in the oil in a deep, non-stick pot for about 5 minutes or until softened. Add the sugo and bring to the boil. Reduce the heat and gently lower the cabbage rolls into the sauce. Quarter the head of cabbage and add to the pot.

> Simmer for an hour over low heat, seasoning to taste, and serve in a deep bowl (with crusty bread if you're especially hungry).

Serves 4

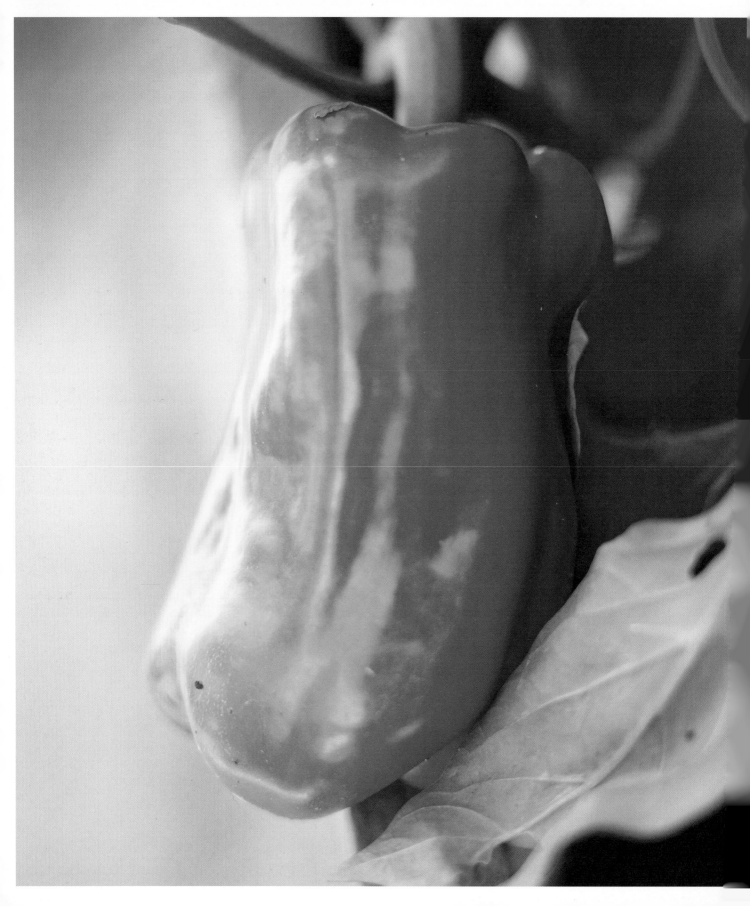

CAPSICUM

'The strangest thing I can say about a capsicum is that my father, a chilli addict, hates them. I've never understood that. Trying to fight someone's food psychology is generally done in vain, and as we grow older, I notice myself becoming more mature. These days I chop it up finely before integrating it into his meals.' —MP

All capsicums start off green, then ripen into another colour once they mature. There are black-, yellow-, orange-, red- and even chocolate-coloured varieties. If you've ever wondered why green capsicums are always much cheaper than red, it's because of the extra vine time they need to mature.

Capsicums are typically a late summer vegetable but in some areas can be harvested into winter. If you have trouble dealing with the glut, slow roast them, then preserve them in good olive oil — a delight to eat on a crusty loaf with a rub of garlic.

Botanical name
Capsicum annuum

Family
Solanaceae (Nightshade family)

Origin
Central and South America

Little Veggie Patch favourite
Sweet Banana

Space needs
Suited to larger pots, but prefer an in-ground veggie patch

Companion plants
Parsley, basil

How to grow
Propagate seeds in individual cells

When to plant
>Zone 1: October–December
>Zone 2: August–November
>Zone 3: August–March
>Zone 4: Any time

Soil preparation
Prepare a rich, free-draining soil with well-rotted manure a fortnight prior to planting.

pH level
5.5–6.5

Position
Hottest part of your veggie patch but sheltered from winds

Spacing
50 cm

Problems
Root-knot nematodes, blossom end rot

CAPSICUM

Sow seeds in individual cells no more than 0.5–1.0 cm deep, then cover with soil and water in. Leave them outdoors during the daytime, bringing them indoors at night. Transplant once the daytime temperatures are regularly surpassing 20ºC, as capsicum doesn't tolerate frost. It is a slow-growing plant that is also slow to form fruit. Be patient.

If you are planting capsicum in a position that is exposed to winds, build or plant some form of windbreak. Corn, for example, will fulfill this purpose perfectly.

Feeding and mulching

Keep up a good level of nitrogen in the soil with fortnightly feeds of liquid seaweed fertiliser. On a couple of occasions during the growing process, incorporate organic matter into the soil to improve resistance to root-knot nematodes.

After transplanting the seedlings, mulch with a 3–5 cm thick layer of pea straw or lucerne hay, then reapply it later in the season.

Watering

After transplanting, the capsicum plants will require watering 2–3 times a week for the first month. Then cut back to once a week to encourage stronger root development.

Water consistently, as under- and overwatering make the fruit prone to blossom end rot.

Harvesting

Capsicums can be harvested green or left to mature into their ripe colour. When picking them, twist until the fruit snaps off, or use scissors to save you the effort as well as avoid damaging the plant.

CARROT

Pulling a carrot out of the ground is still a thrill — it's the closest thing we have to a vegetable lottery. If you ever wanted a vegetable to highlight the origins of our food, there is no greater example than the hugely recognisable and popular carrot. Ask your child to pull one out of your backyard veggie patch and their mind will instantly open.

The carrots you grow will look nothing like the long, fat, waxed things you buy from the supermarket. They will be bent, hooked, curved and stumpy. If you're really lucky, you'll even find two hungry lovers curled around each other in a battle for life.

Carrots can stay in the ground during cooler periods until you are ready to eat them. Your soil will act as a form of storage, saving you from an overdose of vitamin C.

Botanical name
Daucus carota var. *sativus*

Family
Apiaceae (Carrot family)

Origin
Europe, North Africa and Central Asia

Little Veggie Patch favourite
Baby Amsterdam

Space needs
Suited to smaller pots

Companion plants
Radish, onion

How to grow
Sow seed directly into the patch

When to plant
> Zone 1: September–February
> Zone 2: September–May
> Zone 3: February–November
> Zone 4: February–November

Soil preparation
Dig through well-rotted organic matter and manure to create a friable, free-draining soil.

pH level
6.5–7.5

Position
Full sun, following a crop of nitrogen-hungry leafy greens

Spacing
2–5 cm

Create shallow trenches approximately 0.5–1 cm deep, then sprinkle the seeds along the trench line. Brush over the soil, gently firm down and water in. A couple of weeks after germination, thin out the seedlings — cull some seedlings to make sufficient room for the others to grow. Carrot pests are normally attracted to the smell of carrot foliage, which is strongest after thinning, so water plants thoroughly after thinning to dissipate the scent, and do not leave a thinned out crop lying around. Dispose of them properly by adding them to your compost.

Plant carrot and radish seeds together and avoid thinning out. Radishes mature more quickly than carrots, so your harvesting of mature radishes will double up as the thinning out exercise for your carrots. Alternatively, plant carrot seeds in sand so they are better and more evenly spaced.

Feeding and mulching

Avoid adding too much compost and fresh manure, as these can result in split carrots. If you prepare your soil properly, your carrots will only need a monthly application of liquid seaweed fertiliser. Once the carrot foliage is large enough for mulching, use pea straw or lucerne hay to a thickness of 2–3 cm; mulching around tiny germinated seedlings can be a nightmare.

Watering

Even and regular watering is also important to prevent splitting. Water new seedlings 2–3 times a week, but then cut back to once a week, or water as necessary so the soil doesn't completely dry out.

Harvesting

You can harvest carrots early as baby carrots, depending on the variety, or allow them to mature. Use a garden fork to carefully loosen the soil and free the carrots. They can remain in the soil, and will store better if the conditions are cool and not too wet. If the old layer of mulch has broken down too much, protect them from frost with a new layer.

CAULIFLOWER

If you, like us, enjoy a glass or two of wine most nights, chances are your liver is living a pretty awful life. Let's face it, your liver can never, and will never, understand the subtlety of wines matched with food. It also has a reputation for being a little touchy and self-absorbed, so you really need to tread cautiously. But then we eat cauliflower and feel completely at ease.

Cauliflower improves your liver's ability to detoxify. So while we don't condone boozing it up as long as you're eating a head of cauliflower, you may find yourself admitting that, 'Yes, the Chianti was very nice, and I did eat some cauliflower earlier, so I may have one last glass before catching a taxi home, thank you.'

As cauliflower is a brassica, soil and pest preparation are the keys to your crop's success, not to mention a way of justifying that second glass of wine.

Botanical name
Brassica oleracea var. botrytis

Family
Brassicaceae (Mustard family)

Origin
Mediterranean

Little Veggie Patch favourite
Violetta Italia

Space needs
Suited to larger pots, but prefer an in-ground veggie patch

Companion plants
Onion, dill, chamomile

How to grow
Propagate seeds in individual seed cells

When to plant
>Zone 1: February–April
>Zone 2: March–April
>Zone 3: March–April
>Zone 4: March–April

Soil preparation
Prepare soil with a green manure, and incorporate fresh manure and compost into the mix to improve its water-holding ability. Allow the soil to settle down for a couple of weeks before planting.

pH level
6.5–7.5

Position
Full sun, in a well-drained soil. Avoid planting where brassica crops have been grown in the last couple of seasons.

Spacing
60–80 cm

Problems
White cabbage moth, aphids

CAULIFLOWER

Sow seed in individual seed cells at a depth 2–3 times the diameter of the seed, backfill with soil and water in. Keep them indoors at night to avoid frost damage and transplant when the seedlings are 2–3 weeks old.

Cover with fine netting to keep white cabbage moths at bay. If you live in a region that suffers from prolonged frosts, it helps to bend a few outer leaves over the developing heads for protection. Just pin them down with a toothpick.

Feeding and mulching

Water 2–3 times a week for the first month, cutting back to once or twice a week and accommodating any rainfall. Fertilise with liquid seaweed every fortnight after planting.

Cauliflower enjoys a soil that holds moisture without being soggy, so build up the organic matter by adding compost 2–3 times during the planting season and mulching with pea straw or lucerne hay to a depth of 3–5 cm after transplanting.

Harvesting

Cauliflower is ready when the heads are about the size of your two fists put together. This does not apply to monsters or midgets. Harvest in the same fashion as broccoli, by cutting the heads low on the stem. Secondary heads, however, do not regenerate to the same extent, so to avoid attracting pests and diseases, and to prevent further nutrient depletion of your soil, remove the entire plant from the patch once you have harvested the main head.

CELERY

A stick of celery should find its way into nearly every soup or casserole, and even has a place in our cherished Sunday night pasta ragùs. We can't be entirely sure how the latter eventuated, but it follows a regional habit of always adding a stick or two when preparing the sauce. Celery is also an ideal grazing vegetable, a crunchy, peppery snack, and picking individual stems will encourage further growth. A no-brainer, win-win.

Munching on a stick of celery in your backyard is about as primal as you will get to feel in suburban Australia. Let the leafy parts whale from your lips as you chew it with your mouth wide open, much like a roaming herbivore grazer.

Used primarily in contemporary cooking for its stalks, celery also produces edible seeds that are high in calcium and thought to help arthritis.

Celery is generally considered a cooler weather crop, but there are types that thrive in warmer weather.

Botanical name
Apium graveolens var. dulce

Family
Apiaceae (Carrot family)

Origin
Europe and Asia

Little Veggie Patch favourite
Amsterdam

Space needs
Suited to smaller pots

Companion plant
Tomato

How to grow
Propagate in seed trays

When to plant
>Zone 1: March–December
>Zone 2: April–December
>Zone 3: March–October
>Zone 4: February–September

Soil preparation
Add organic matter before planting to improve fertility and the soil's ability to hold water.

pH level
5.8–6.8

Position
Full sun to part shade in a well-drained soil. Don't plant near carrots, as they are not great friends. It could get awkward.

Spacing
30–40 cm

Problems
Snails and slugs

Before planting in seed trays, soak the seeds in water to aid germination. Sow at a depth 2–3 times the seed's diameter, backfill and water in. Celery is slow to germinate, so don't become despondent if there is no growth, even after 2 weeks.

When transplanting, make sure the roots are planted deeply enough, as they will need to hold the plant's own weight as it matures.

The stalks have a tendency to splay out as they grow, so loosely tying them together with soft twine or a rubber band will help the plant form a more upright growth habit. Mounding soil or compost up against the base will also help stabilise it.

Blanching the stalks makes them more tender and the flavour less peppery and sharp. Wrap the base of the plant with thick paper or cardboard so it blocks out the light, and secure with twine — don't use plastic, as the humidity will build up and the plant will become susceptible to pests.

Celery benefits from shading, so plant taller crops around it.

Feeding and mulching

Celery has a high demand for nutrients, so apply a liquid seaweed fertiliser every fortnight. After transplanting, mulch with lucerne hay or pea straw to a depth of 3–5 cm.

Watering

Consistent watering is important for developing watery but crisp stalks. When mature, celery likes to be watered twice a week. Before the seedlings are a month old they will need an extra water each week.

Harvesting

Celery is a perfect grazing vegetable that can be picked stalk by stalk. Snap the outer stalks with your hand, or use a knife to prevent dislodging the whole plant. Constant harvesting will help generate new growth.

USING RECYCLED
MATERIALS IN
YOUR VEGGIE PATCH

We love going to the tip to hunt for treasure, and find it unnatural to pass through without taking a peek. Strolling through the salvage shop is like a visit to Ikea — you go with the intention of purchasing one item you need and leave with many that you probably didn't. We are not hoarders by nature, but there are some bargains that are just irresistible — the skateboard stashed in the corner of a bedroom, a $2 investment that paid for itself on its maiden voyage down the hallway, and of course, the empty wine rack that doesn't hold wine as long as it takes to drink it. These items and many more, now living meaningful second lives, have been saved from landfill, becoming small recycling success stories.

Recycling success stories are in evidence throughout the vegetable garden, too. Composting and worm-farming are two pure forms of recycling whose value to the veggie garden is unquestionable, while the ideology behind no-dig gardening encourages the use of whatever materials you have on hand. Other common examples of recycling include using fruit tree prunings to build trellises; plastic bottles to incubate seedlings; and toilet rolls and egg cartons to propagate seeds.

When you want to give your veggie patch a touch of the X factor, the salvage shop is the best place to start. A general rule of thumb is that the closer your tip is to the city centre (or a place where the cool kids hang out), the lesser the quality and value of the bargain. Recycling is big business these days, and vintage stores tend to dip their beaks in first, so the further out of town you go, the greater chance you have of striking gold.

You are after materials that can either be reconstructed in a practical sense or give your vegetable garden character, but preferably both. Try to keep the materials in theme with what you are hoping to achieve. For example, use a vintage bike as a feature or a rustic watering can to hold herbs — these will provide a rustic, cottage feel that your adult friends will admire.

But this is more of a kids' activity, so you are left to their devices. Your kids may sense that the 'cottage' theme screams old and conservative, so you will have to adapt to their tastes here. Chances are they're going through a sci-fi phase, so they're going to drool over the retro ski boots, which remind them of the stormtroopers in *Star Wars*, and the fluorescent pink and green ski poles doubling up as life sabers.

When constructing your theme for the kids, if you find that their tastes deviate too greatly from yours, focus on creating a small section of the garden in their chosen theme to give them complete ownership of it. This will then allow some space for your cottage garden elsewhere.

Building a golf-club trellis

Create a tee-pee with golf clubs over the spot where you will grow your climbing veggie plant. Using recycled clubs will give you a practical, vintage-looking trellis in your veggie patch, as well as providing an early introduction to a sport that is relaxing, challenging and insanely frustrating.

This activity requires:
> recycled golf clubs (as many as you like, but 3–6 is ideal)
> cable ties
> binding cord

1

Sourcing the clubs will involve a trip to the salvage shop at your local tip or exploring the dustiest, dirtiest corner of your garage where your Grandad's 1950s golf clubs reside. Try to keep wooden drivers and iron clubs in groups, as they keep the look consistent and will be similar lengths.

2

Start forming the tee-pee, ensuring the clubs are pretty evenly spaced.

3

Bind the top of the tee-pee together with cable ties.

4

Cover the cable ties with binding cord.

5

Plant your seedlings.

CHILLI

We often wonder why the first people to eat chillies decided to eat them again. And continue to wonder why so many of us, knowing the ramifications, eat them again and again and again. Humans, the most developed of primates, we're told, have a tendency for this sort of behaviour. Maybe there is some instinctively acquired knowledge of chilli's innumerable health benefits, from lowering blood pressure to aiding intestinal diseases? Others put it down to a health placebo, a rush, almost an aphrodisiac, that drives chilli users to the edge.

'My father, a seasoned chilli user, is representative of the chilli community. He grows chilli almost exclusively, adding it to most foods, including his morning toast, and he is now exempt from the chilli mouth sting. He rates them based on the heat his head emits. As he is a fair-headed and fair-skinned man, it is not difficult to know when the stuff is good — his face drips with sweat and his eyes tear up as if to say, "Oooh yeeaaaaahhhhhh!"' —MP

An annual plant that can perform as a perennial in warmer climates (it needs a good cut back after harvest), chilli's power is usually in a direct and proportionate relationship to its size and colour — red and small being the most powerful. However, there are exceptions, and these can only be discovered the hard way.

Botanical name
Capsicum annuum, C. baccatum, C. chinense, C. pubescens

Family name
Solanaceae (Nightshade family)

Origin
Central and South America

Little Veggie Patch favourite
The damned hot little ones that Michelo's sister-in-law's father's cousin brought back from Sicily — or was it Abruzzo — in 1952. No, the summer of 1953.

Space needs
Suited to smaller pots

Companion plants
Basil, parsley

How to grow
Propagate indoors in seed trays

When to plant
> Zone 1: October–December
> Zone 2: September–December
> Zone 3: August–March
> Zone 4: April–July

Soil preparation
The soil should be rich and free-draining. Integrate compost and well-rotted animal manure a fortnight before planting. Chillies will also benefit from an application of lime.

pH level
6.5–7.5

Position
Sunny, hot position in free draining soil. Don't plant where hungry crops, such as brassicas, were previously growing.

Spacing
30 cm

Problems
Fruit flies

Sow seeds in individual cells no more than 0.5–1.0 cm deep, then cover with soil and water in. Leave them outdoors during the daytime, but bring them indoors at night. Transplant chillies once the daytime temperatures are regularly surpassing 20°C, as they don't tolerate frost.

Sensitive to cold and slow-growing, chilli plants require ideal conditions in which to thrive, so be patient with their progress. When the conditions are right, with high daytime temperatures and the soil temperature closing in on 20°C, their growth rate improves significantly.

Feeding and mulching

Ensure there is sufficient calcium in the soil (so your plants will be less likely to develop blossom end rot) and keep your watering consistent and the level of organic matter in the soil high.

After transplanting the seedlings, mulch with a 3–5 cm layer of pea straw or lucerne hay. You will need to reapply this later in the season.

If you remove the plant after harvesting, practise crop rotation and avoid planting it in the same spot year after year.

Watering

As your chilli plants should occupy the hottest position in your veggie patch, irrigation is the key, so keep watering regular and consistent. Water your seedlings 2–3 times a week for the first month, then give the mature plants one good soaking per week to encourage strong root development.

Harvesting

Pull chillies off the plant by hand, or cut off with scissors. Successive harvesting will encourage further growth. Both the flavour and heat develop as the fruit ripens, so pick your chillies to suit your taste and heat requirements.

If you live in a warmer region, prune back your plants at the end of the harvest and they should survive the winter.

Nonna's Kitchen

Chilli oil

1 prolific chilli plant
500 ml malt or brown vinegar
good-quality extra-virgin olive oil

> Harvest the chilli plant by clipping off the chillies with scissors.

> Still using the scissors, cut the chillies into 0.5 cm pieces and place the pieces in a bowl.

> Fill the bowl with vinegar to just cover the chillies.

> Cover and leave for 24 hours.

> Drain the chillies and put them in a sterilised jar. Cover the chillies with oil.

> The flavour and strength of the chilli oil will intensify over time.

Serve with your Sunday night ragù.

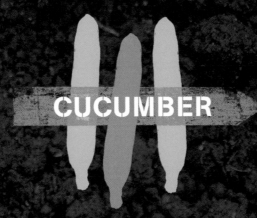

CUCUMBER

Mutual happiness is the process of taking the first season's pick of cucumber to a mate's bar in Northcote. He's happy, for he has the crucial ingredient for some of the finest summer beverages; we're ecstatic, because cucumbers routinely come off the vine in truckloads, and fine summer beverages seem a more than equitable barter exchange. For this reason the first cucumber pick is highly anticipated.

Cucumber is a prolific climber, and when space is scarce, should be incorporated vertically into your garden. If space is not at a premium, the vines of the plant can act as a natural mulch, interplanted among larger crops, such as eggplant or sweetcorn.

FYI: Gerkins are not just immature cucumbers but in fact a specific variety belonging to the same species.

Botanical name
Cucumis sativus

Family
Cucurbitaceae (Gourd family)

Origin
North India

Little Veggie Patch favourite
Marketmore

Space needs
Suited to larger pots, but prefer an in-ground veggie patch

Companion plants
Corn, eggplant

How to grow
Sow directly into the patch

When to plant
>Zone 1: October–December
>Zone 2: September–January
>Zone 3: August–March
>Zone 4: February–September

Soil preparation
Prepare a well-drained, moderately fertile soil. Mix in compost and well-rotted animal manure a fortnight prior to planting.

pH level
6.5–7.0

Position
Sunny spot in well-drained soil. Plant at the base of your eggplant or corn. Alternatively, consider growing the plant on a trellis to save space.

Spacing
1 m

Problem
Powdery mildew

CUCUMBER

Sow seed directly into the soil, at a depth 2–3 times the diameter of the seed, then backfill and water in. If conditions are unseasonably cool, it is best to propagate in seed trays and transplant the seedlings when the temperature heats up.

Once the plant begins to mature, pinch out the growth tips to encourage it to branch out and produce more fruit.

Feeding and mulching

After the seedlings have established, mulch with a 3–5 cm layer of pea straw or lucerne hay to lock in moisture and keep the soil temperature constant. If you choose to let the vine travel at ground level, mulch also prevents the fruit from rotting on the ground.

Feed your plants fortnightly with an application of liquid seaweed fertiliser.

Watering

Seedlings will need to be watered 2–3 times a week for the first month. Cut back to once a week, or twice when conditions are hot. Regular watering, especially when the plant is fruiting, will ensure flowers set and produce juicy fruit.

Harvesting

When harvesting, avoid pulling on the fruit and stressing the plant. Twisting the fruit in one direction until it breaks off works well, but cutting is best. Picking the fruit will encourage further production.

EGGPLANT

Did you know that eggplant contains higher levels of nicotine than any other edible plant? Absolutely true. If you consume 10 kg of eggplant, you may as well have smoked a cigarette. That's quite a compliment for a cigarette, but we digress…

The spikes on the neck of an eggplant can be truly annoying. If the ability to retain information, such as what hurts to touch, is not your strong point, every time you venture to the patch to fetch an eggplant you may return agitated and cursing the mystery of evolution.

Before cooking eggplant, salt its flesh, as it will sweat out the bitterness of the fruit and reduce its level of absorption, saving you money on olive oil and helping you maintain a healthy cholesterol level. This process is known as degorging.

The skinny varieties of eggplant, typified by the Lebanese variety, fruit earlier in the season, so for a staggered harvest, it's a good idea to incorporate different plants in your patch.

Botanical name
Solanum melongena

Family
Solanaceae (Nightshade family)

Origin
India

Little Veggie Patch favourite
Long Purple

Space needs
Suited to larger pots, but prefer an in-ground veggie patch

Companion plant
Cucumber

How to grow
Propagate in seed trays

When to plant
>Zone 1: September–November
>Zone 2: August–December
>Zone 3: August–March
>Zone 4: Any time

Soil preparation
A couple of weeks prior to planting, prepare the soil by incorporating a high level of organic matter, such as compost and well-rotted animal manure.

pH level
6.0–7.0

Position
Choose a sunny, hot position in free-draining soil. Eggplant will appreciate the heat.

Spacing
40–60 cm

Problems
Fruit flies, root rot

EGGPLANT

Sow seed in trays indoors and transplant the seedlings once conditions are warm, well after the last frost. Sow at a depth 2–3 times the diameter of the seed, then backfill and water in. Seedlings are slow to develop, so don't be stressed if germination doesn't occur for 2 weeks or more.

Feeding and mulching

Mulch well to retain moisture, which is especially important in the warmer spots of your patch. Apply a 3–5 cm layer of pea straw or lucerne hay. Keep the stem of your plant exposed, as building up mulch around it will make it susceptible to root rot. Feed once a month with a slow-release organic fertiliser or liquid seaweed extract.

In warmer regions the plants can stay in the ground and act as perennials, producing fruit over a number of growing seasons.

Watering

Water regularly to keep your plants happy and stress-free. Water 2–3 times a week while the plants are establishing, then cut back to one good soaking every week to encourage deep root growth.

Harvesting

When harvesting, wear gloves or simply take more care than we do — eggplants can have ferocious spikes. Twisting will snap off the fruit, but it's best to use scissors to cut them off. Younger, smaller eggplants will be tastier, sweeter and not as bitter as older, larger fruit.

FENNEL

The flavour of fennel can prove a little challenging for kids. Its distinct aniseed taste is most powerful when the vegetable is raw, but much more subtle and kid-friendly when it is cooked. While fennel can be a sharp accent in a simple green salad, a favoured dish of ours is a slow-roasted whole chicken, accompanied by large chunks of fennel and seasoned with lemon wedges and thyme in a stock of white wine. Please do yourself a favour and try it.

Fennel is yet another vegetable that doubles up as a coarse word in Italian, this one, however, more offensive than the others.

Fennel is a perennial plant that should self-seed year after year. If space allows, designate a special spot for this problem child, as it doesn't often get along with the other kids. In small spaces, and in small numbers, everyone is much more tolerant of each other.

Known for its digestive qualities, fennel will help neutralise the 'windy vegetables', such as cabbage and Jerusalem artichoke.

Botanical name
Foeniculum vulgare var. *azoricum*

Family
Apiaceae (Carrot family)

Origin
Southern Europe

Little Veggie Patch favourite
Florence

Space needs
Suited to smaller pots

How to grow
Sow seed directly into the patch

When to plant
> Zone 1: March–December
> Zone 2: March–November
> Zone 3: August–September
> Zone 4: March–August

Soil preparation
While fennel will tolerate different soil conditions, keep the soil loose and friable to allow ease of growth. It prefers a well-drained soil that is prepared with compost and green manure a couple of weeks prior to sowing.

pH level
6.5–7.5

Position
Will tolerate part shade. Most herbs will not mind its antisocial behaviour.

Spacing
20–30 cm

Problems
Generally pest- and disease-free

FENNEL

Sow seed directly at a depth of approximately 0.5 to 1 cm, backfill with soil and water in. Thin out the seedlings once they have germinated, allowing space for the remaining ones to grow. Avoid sowing fennel while conditions are hot, as it tends to bolt to seed.

Feeding and mulching

To accelerate the development of the root stems and avoid stressing the plant, feed fortnightly with a liquid seaweed fertiliser. Stressed plants tend to bolt to seed. Mulch with a 3–5 cm layer of pea straw or lucerne hay when the seedlings are 2–3 weeks old.

Watering

Water new seedlings 2–3 times a week for the first month. Water regularly thereafter so the soil won't dry out. Whether this is once or twice a week will depend on the seasonal conditions.

Harvesting

Pick fennel when they are young and about the size of a fist. Larger, older plants will be stringy and tough. Use a knife to cut the plant at the base of the root or pull the whole plant out of the ground.

GARLIC

Garlic is too important a cooking ingredient not to be growing in your veggie patch. While it is difficult to attain the bulb size we are accustomed to in the supermarket, what home-grown garlic may lack in size it more than compensates in bite and flavour. And that is what home-growing is all about. When chopping garlic, it's literally impossible to avoid smelling your fingers incessantly until the scent completely dissipates.

While most of us confine the use of garlic to its bulb, the stem and leaves of the plant also possess the distinct flavour of garlic but in a less aggressive form, perfect for stir-frying or sautéing alongside stronger flavours.

In the garden, garlic is a good companion plant for most vegetables. It is also used as an organic additive to natural pest treatments.

Garlic has medicinal benefits too. It is believed to be antibacterial and antiviral, while empirical evidence shows it to be highly antisexual.

Botanical name
Allium sativum

Family
Amaryllidaceae (Onion family)

Origin
Central Asia

Little Veggie Patch favourite
Melbourne Market

Space needs
Suited to smaller pots

Companion plants
Most vegetables, but especially the carrot

How to grow
Plant cloves

When to plant
> Zone 1: April–May
> Zone 2: April–June
> Zone 3: May–July
> Zone 4: June–July

Soil preparation
Prepare a free-draining, friable soil with compost. A week prior to planting, turn your soil over with compost to a depth of 20 cm. If the soil is compacted, the bulbs won't grow well.

pH level
6.5–7.5

Position
A sunny position among other vegetables

Spacing
10–15 cm

Problems
Generally pest- and disease-free

Break off the sprouting cloves from the bulb and sow with the sprout pointing skywards, at a depth of 3–5 cm. Firm down the soil after planting, as the root growth can sometimes push the clove out of the soil, then water in. Avoid planting garlic that has been purchased from the supermarket, as it is likely to have been imported and could introduce diseases to your soil. Purchase bulbs that are certified organic.

The bulb will reach its optimum size in more friable soil and be inhibited by compacted soil, so keep foot traffic away from your garlic.

One trick for improving bulb size is to tie a knot in the foliage a month before you anticipate harvesting. This is meant to transfer growing energy from the foliage to the bulb.

Feeding and mulching

Once the seedlings are 2–3 weeks old, mulch the ground around your garlic with a layer of pea straw or lucerne hay. Garlic likes regular feeding, so apply a dosage of liquid seaweed extract once a fortnight.

Watering

Young garlic will tolerate a relatively high level of moisture, especially during the germination period; however, cut back on watering as the plant matures. Initially you will need to water at least 3 times a week, but later on, twice a week at most. Before harvesting, when the foliage begins to turn yellow, cut back significantly on watering to dry and harden the bulbs.

Harvesting

Gently lift the plant from the ground in the same way you would gently pull your sister's hair if you were trying to annoy her. Alternatively, use a fork, avoiding damaging the bulb. Hang in a warm, dark place so the garlic can mature and dry. Once it is dry, remove any remaining soil from the bulb.

For self-seeding bulbs over the following seasons, let garlic go to seed. However, most garlic is sown from the previous year's bulbs, so consider saving your best for planting the following season.

HERBS

Truly, one of our great hates is forking out $4 for a sprig of basil or rosemary or thyme, wasting time and fuel getting to the supermarket, using a quarter of the bunch and then eventually ditching the rest. Our hearts sink as we imagine all those wasted multiples of $4, along with the unnecessary fuel kilometres.

If you're living in a share-house and looking for a good house-bonding activity, try scouring the streets for 'legal tender' rather than venturing to the supermarket for your herbs. After each excursion, compile a map of the herb variety and the location from which it was sourced. If you're ever caught crossing the line, where 'legal tender' may become 'illegal tender', simply state that you are providing an experimental pruning service from which you wish to derive commercial success in the future. This should confuse your neighbour enough for you to escape verbal punishment.

Whatever the scale or ambition of your veggie garden endeavours, herbs are so easy to grow and beneficial on so many levels for the rest of your crops, you should incorporate them sparingly throughout your garden. Relatively pest-free themselves, their scent and flower colour will help repel harmful pests from your annual crops while using those same weapons to attract pollinators.

Most herbs are perennial plants that are harvested by picking the sprigs or leaves, which then regenerate. While most go dormant during the colder months, there will be enough growth on your established plants to satisfy all your cooking requirements, saving you costly and unnecessary trips to the supermarket, not to mention any neighbourhood pruning services.

Little Veggie Patch favourite
Spicy Globe Basil and
flat-leafed parsley

Space needs
Suited to smaller pots

Companion plants
Most vegetables benefit from
nearby herbs.

How to grow
Sow seed directly, or purchase
seedlings and transplant to
your patch.

When to plant
Refer table overleaf

Soil preparation
Mix through compost and
organic matter to create a
fertile, friable soil.

pH level
6.5–8.0

Position
Full sun preferable, but part
shade manageable

Spacing
30–50 cm

Problems
Generally pest- and disease-free

Herbs are hardy perennials that will survive in most soil types, and most are self-seeding and relatively simple to grow, so they will regenerate new plants by themselves. Alternatively, get into the habit of collecting seed from your herbs and replant them the following season.

When first planting herbs it is best to start from seedlings and water in well after transplanting. Wait a month or more before harvesting.

Feeding and mulching

Apply liquid seaweed fertiliser every 2 or 4 weeks. After transplanting, mulch with pea straw or lucerne hay to a depth of 3–5 cm. Repeat when necessary.

Watering

To establish stronger root growth, keep your herbs well-watered during their infancy. Two to three times a week will suffice. Once they mature, most herbs will be hardy enough to get by on rainfall alone, but will benefit from a deep watering if conditions are dry.

Harvesting

Your herbs will be ready for harvesting once the plant is at a mature size and at a point when picking doesn't greatly affect its ability to photosynthesise. Wait until your herb seedlings have been in for at least a month.

Herbs are best harvested by using a sharp pair of scissors to snip off segments of leaf growth at the base of the stem. The harvesting process and seasonal cut-backs will prevent your herbs from becoming woody and result in bushier plants.

When to plant herbs

	Zone 1	Zone 2	Zone 3	Zone 4
Basil (annual)	October–January	September–Feb	Any time	September–December
Chives	September–April	September–May	Any time	Any time
Coriander (annual)	October–June	September–June	April–November	April–July
Dill	September–November	August–January	March–August	June
Mint	September–December	August–November	August–November	April–July
Oregano	October–March	September–May	August–May	May–August
Parsley	October–March	September–May	August–May	May–August
Rosemary	October–March	September–May	August–May	May–August
Thyme	October–March	September–May	August–May	May–August

STOP
LOSING
YOUR TOOLS!

Pipe cutters come in two colours — bright orange and black. No doubt the first generation of pipe cutters was made in bright orange, a colour chosen by a morally driven company to prevent buyers from losing them. The problem was that with a product so soundly constructed and nearly impossible to lose on a worksite, sales suffered. When the company's board, on the verge of liquidation, next met to discuss its new sales drive, their strategy was to produce the second generation of pipe cutters, this time in black. The success of their sales strategy lies in our toolbox, where we have one blunt pair of orange cutters, purchased in 2004, and four new black ones. While we don't often lose pipe cutters on worksites, we regularly lose them in the toolbox and purchase more.

A pair of pipe cutters is one example of many tools that tend to be misplaced on the worksite or at home when gardening. Playing hide and seek with shovels leaning up against fences or rakes lying under piles of leaves gets tiresome and expensive. As much as we admire innovative sales strategies, it was time to put an end to this nonsense and paint our tools in an easily recognisable colour, thus saving the associated frustration and cost of misplacing them.

Painting anything is an activity that the kids will jump at, especially when that anything is something that didn't really need to be painted in the first place. If, for some reason, your kids aren't taken by this activity, simply place all the tools you wish to be painted in a contained room with a tin of brightly coloured paint and paint brushes, then say to your kids: 'Kids, whatever you do, please don't go in that room and paint my tools.' The job is as good as done.

Painting your garden tools

Painting is an activity most adults hate and yet all kids love. So by involving the kids in this activity, we are achieving a win-win outcome. Here we use child-friendly water-based paint, but for a more durable finish adults could use enamel paint.

For this activity you will require the following materials:

> tin of bright water-based paint

> paint brushes

> drop sheet or old newspaper

> enthusiastic child painters

1

Hold a paint conference with your kids and ask them to decide on their favourite colour. If by chance it happens to be black or brown, start a discussion on the Wiggles, then ask them to reassess.

Gather the timber-handled tools that commonly get misplaced — all shovels, rakes, garden forks. In fact, just get all your tools.

2

You don't want to paint your garage or grass the same colour — imagine the problems now — so protect the ground with old sheets or newspaper.

4

Now give the tools a splash of colour!

When painting long-handled tools, you can also dig them into the ground for stability.

Once the paint has dried, test the effectiveness of the activity by playing a game of hide and seek with your new tools.

LEEK

Part of the onion (Amaryllidaceae) family, leek is a hardy vegetable that can be successfully grown in most climates. It can be distinguished from the onion by its broad, flat foliage. Leeks can stay in the ground for up to 12 months without deteriorating.

If you wonder why leeks tend to contain soil within their layers, it is because growers mound up the soil above the plants' roots (known as trenching) as part of the blanching process, which enhances their tenderness and flavour.

Great in soups (most famously with potato) and quiches, leeks can also be used in salads as a less intense substitute for onion.

Botanical name
Allium ampeloprasum var. *porrum*

Family
Amaryllidaceae (Onion family)

Origin
Western Asia and Europe

Little Veggie Patch favourite
American Flag

Space needs
Suited to smaller pots

Companion plants
Carrots

How to grow
Propagate in seed trays

When to plant
>Zone 1: September–March
>Zone 2: August–April
>Zone 3: January–March
>Zone 4: February–March

Soil preparation
Leeks can handle most soil types, but it should be free-draining, with added compost.

pH level
6.5–7.5

Position
Shade-tolerant, so plant in a less than ideal spot in the patch.

Spacing
10–15 cm

Problems
Snails and slugs

LEEK

Don't over-fertilise the soil prior to planting, as this will make your leeks more susceptible to frost damage. Transplant the seedlings a month after germination, or sow direct into the veggie patch at a depth of 1 cm when the temperature is consistently above 7°C. Leeks take up to 2 years to develop seed heads, so if you want to collect the seeds, you'll need to be patient.

Blanch the stem by continuously mounding soil around it as it grows, which will starve it of sunlight and result in a more tender and flavoursome crop. However, be careful not to overdo the mounding when the plants are young, as you may rot the entire plant.

Feeding and mulching

Leeks enjoy a good layer of mulch to keep the soil temperature consistent. Use pea straw or lucerne hay to a depth of 5 cm. These plants don't like to be overfed, so just add some slow-release organic fertiliser when planting.

Watering

Seedlings will need watering 2–3 times a week for the first month. Thereafter make sure you water your leeks regularly so the soil doesn't completely dry out.

Harvesting

Leeks can be left in the ground for up to a year before harvesting without losing their flavour or deteriorating; however, in warmer climates, be careful about storing them in the ground — monitor how they are keeping with regular taste tests.

Pull them from the ground when they are ready to harvest — that is, at a thickness you deem fit, anywhere between an adult thumb and a child's wrist. Leeks have deep and strong root systems, so you may need a garden fork to loosen the soil around them. Alternatively, cut off the stems and they will regenerate for round two.

LEMON

A lemon tree, a must for any household, is a common sight in Australian backyards, where it can enjoy a hot, sunny position. Why lemons are actually sold in supermarkets surprises us. Walk down any street, in any suburb, in any city, and you will come across any number of plants, usually with fruit on them. Two words: 'legal tender'.

Urinating around a lemon tree provides a tonic of water, salt and minerals, much like that of an organic fertiliser, and considering it's a far better weeing experience than using a standard toilet, there is no reason why your tree should be nutrient-deficient. Just don't overdo it by inviting your workmates over every Friday night for drinks and citrus weeing.

Lemon trees, like all citrus, are evergreen plants that should have shiny, healthy leaves all year round, and fruit twice, in autumn and spring. It is advisable to plant a thornless variety such as 'Eureka' to remove any danger from the harvest. Lemon trees are fantastic to grow in pots; make sure you use good quality potting mix and consider a dwarf variety. Also be aware that when planting full-growing varieties in pots, limiting the space will essentially 'dwarf' the tree and control its size.

Botanical name
Citrus limon

Family
Rutaceae (Citrus family)

Origin
India

Little Veggie Patch favourite
Eureka

Space needs
Can be grown in larger pots but prefers being in-ground

Companion plants
Nasturtium, marigold, lavender

Where to plant
Loves heat and humidity, so as long as the soil drains well, it will grow anywhere Australia-wide. For those living in cooler climates, choose your position carefully — warm and sheltered is preferable.

How to grow
Transplant a bagged or potted adolescent tree

When to plant
Spring is the best time to plant.
> Zone 1: September–November
> Zone 2: September–November
> Zone 3: October–December
> Zone 4: October–December

Soil preparation
Dig through compost and fresh manure to a depth of 20–30 cm, allowing the soil a fortnight to settle (otherwise backfill with compost and well-rotted manure when planting).

pH level
5.5–6.5

Position
Full sun, in free-draining soil, as citrus hate to get their feet wet

Spacing
3–4 m

Problems
Gall wasp, leaf miners

When planting citrus in pots, we recommend you re-pot every 2–3 years with fresh potting mix, moving up a pot size if necessary.

The major pest of the lemon tree is the gall wasp, which can be found throughout Australia. Avoid over-fertilising your tree, or you'll make it a more attractive proposition for nesting gall wasps. Once they're established in your tree the only option is to cut off the affected limbs and dispose of them properly in general waste, not your compost pile. Gall wasp shouldn't kill your tree, but it will severely stunt its growth and reduce its fruit production, so living with the pest and then drastically pruning back the branches every 4–5 years is recommended.

Before you buy, check whether the tree is root-bound by gently pulling on the trunk to see if it comes out of the pot easily. If it does not budge without considerable effort, move on. Avoid buying a plant that is flowering or fruiting, as this is an indication of stress. If you do buy a plant that has flowers or fruit, prune them off after planting.

Also look out for 'J' roots (roots doubling back on themselves) or knots in the root system. These imperfections can cause problems several years down the track, when the tree literally ends up strangling itself. Many nurseries will tie up stock on display, so as a check untie the tree and see if it stands upright under its own weight. If the tree falls over, it most likely has an unbalanced root structure, so move on.

When planting, dig a hole twice the width of the root ball but a little shallower than its height so you can mound the soil around the rest of the roots and ensure good drainage. Before positioning the plant, moisten the hole with about 10 litres of water so it penetrates the surrounding soil. Position the tree, then backfill with soil, creating a furrow that directs water to the plant's roots. Gently firm down the soil, apply a handful of slow-release organic fertiliser and water in thoroughly.

Be careful not to disturb the root structure as you plant, however if the tree is root-bound you may need to untangle the roots and prune them.

Feeding and mulching

Feed with a high-nitrogen fertiliser at the beginning of spring and the end of summer. Mulch well beneath the canopy of the tree, applying a thick 10 cm layer of pea straw or lucerne hay. Always keep grass, particularly creeping varieties, at a safe distance from the tree.

Compared to their in-ground cousins, trees in pots tend to require fertiliser and nutrients, such as magnesium, more often.

Watering

Young lemon trees need decent water in order to establish. Water 2–3 times a week over the first month, then cut back to once a week, except when the tree is fruiting, when it will appreciate extra water. Be careful to monitor the rainfall — citrus don't like being overwatered, and won't mind if the soil dries out at times.

Pruning

Prune in late winter or early spring. If your tree is becoming badly infected with gall wasp, you may need to give it a hard prune.

Espaliering citrus requires a different approach to that of deciduous varieties. Instead of training 3–4 horizontal branches, prune to create a full wall of branches that soak up heat and sunlight. For this reason, it is better if the trellis structure for citrus is a tight grid rather than individual wires.

Harvesting

Pick the fruit when it is ripe by twisting and pulling it off the tree. Fruit will keep well on the tree without rotting, and will fall when ready. The fruit developing from a pale to a darker yellow is a sign the fruit is getting ripe.

LETTUCE

Varieties of lettuce — classified as hearting, non-hearting, butterhead or cos types — grow all year round in all climates. Most varieties are easy to grow and self-seeding, and will regenerate as you graze and pick leaves.

As is the case with your fresh herbs, there should be no reason to venture to the supermarket to spend a fortune on lettuce leaves, and unfortunately in this case, helping yourself to 'legal tender' is not a viable option.

In the veggie garden, there is no task simpler or nicer than collecting a salad bowl full of fresh green leaves. A full garden will provide a variety of taste, texture and colour. The bitterness and spice of rocket along with a broken heart of radicchio goes hand in hand with Sunday night ragu.

Botanical name
Lactuca sativa

Family
Asteraceae (Daisy family)

Origin
Asia

Little Veggie Patch favourite
Red Chicory

Space needs
Suited to smaller pots

Companion plants
Radish, bean, carrot

How to grow
Sow directly into the patch

When to plant
>Zone 1: September–May
>Zone 2: Any time
>Zone 3: Any time
>Zone 4: February–November

Soil preparation
Prepare with compost and well-rotted manure and allow the soil to settle for 1–2 weeks before planting. Fresh manure has a tendency to burn younger lettuce seedlings, so incorporating a green manure in your soil as part of the preparation is also ideal.

pH level
6.5–7.5

Position
Full sun, but will tolerate some shade

Spacing
20 cm

Problems
Snails and slugs, powdery mildew

Sow seeds directly into the soil at a depth between 0.5 and 1 cm, then thin out once the seeds have germinated. Most lettuce seeds are tiny, so mix your seeds with coarse sand and use the broadcast method to sprinkle the mix over the designated spot. Cover lightly with soil, then pat down and water. Don't plant your seeds too deeply, as germination will suffer as a result.

Stagger your planting to ensure a regular harvest of salad.

Shading may be required for some of the more delicate varieties. Try planting your lettuce under larger crops.

Feeding and mulching

Your plants will enjoy fortnightly, even weekly, applications of liquid fertiliser. To lock in moisture and provide the soil with organic matter as it breaks down, mulch the ground well with lucerne hay or pea straw to a depth of 3–5 cm.

Watering

Water your seedlings daily for the first 2 weeks, then cut back to 2–3 times a week. As most lettuce varieties need more regular watering than other crops, you may need to provide water in addition to that provided by your drip system.

Remember that watering in the heat of the day may cause the plants to burn, while watering late at night will attract pests, so it is best to water in the morning. Plants stressed by heat or inconsistent watering will bolt to seed and become bitter.

Harvesting

Pick non-hearting lettuces from the outer leaves, and allow the inner, younger growth to mature. Pick hearting lettuce varieties whole when they are ready. Cut them at the base, leaving the roots in the soil. These will then sprout again, however the second crop tends to be more bitter.

LIME

In southern Australia, limes, unlike lemons, are notoriously hard to grow and incredibly expensive. We have a small pipe dream of planting an urban orchard of lime trees and then monopolising the lime market of Melbourne's bars and restaurants. While a successful Melbourne lime orchard will be a tough challenge, we have seen firsthand proof of prolific lime trees in Melbourne, always the 'Tahitian' variety, some almost burdened with fruit. On our list of things to do is to study these trees and their surrounding environment, then mimic these exact conditions in our orchard.

The warmer your climate, the more success you will have growing prolific lime trees. They prefer hot, humid conditions and dislike frosts, so if you live in a cooler climate, you'll need to choose a variety that is more frost-sensitive, and even provide frost protection. An alternative to a fruiting variety is the kaffir lime (*Citrus hystrix*), which is used primarily for its leaves. Picking its leaves will keep the tree small, making it suitable for small spaces or pot growing.

Lime has a more dynamic flavour, with more pinch than a lemon, and is a preferred ingredient in many drinks and dishes. And yet again and again we are short-changed with a wedge of lemon, the poor man's substitute for lime, in our gin!

Botanical name
Citrus aurantifolia

Family
Rutaceae (Citrus family)

Origin
South-East Asia

Little Veggie Patch favourite
Tahitian

Space needs
Can be grown in larger pots but prefers being in-ground

Companion plants
Nasturtium, marigold, lavender

How to grow
Transplant a bagged or potted adolescent tree

Where to plant
Will grow prolifically in hot, humid regions, with limited success in cooler regions. Northern Australia and the east coast are ideal.

When to plant
>Zone 1: September–November
>Zone 2: September–November
>Zone 3: October–December
>Zone 4: October–December

Soil preparation
Likes a fertile soil, high in nitrogen, with especially good drainage. Prepare your soil with fresh manure and compost a fortnight prior to planting, or backfill with compost and well-rotted manure when planting.

pH level
5.5–6.5

Position
Full sun, lots of heat. Espaliering is advantageous.

Spacing
2–4 m

Problems
Whiteflies, aphids

Asian cooking, particularly Thai, incorporates lime to counteract spicy flavours. In South America, limes are popular and widely grown. Brazil's national cocktail, the caipirinha, is a fine summer drink made with lime, sugar and rum, but beware — you will pay handsomely for it at a trendy bar.

As when buying a lemon tree, avoid buying a plant that is flowering or fruiting, as this is an indication of stress. If you do buy a plant that has flowers or fruit, prune them off after planting.

When planting, dig a hole twice the width of the root ball but a little shallower than its height so you can mound the soil around the rest of the roots and ensure good drainage. Before positioning the plant, moisten the hole with about 10 litres of water so that it penetrates the surrounding soil. Position the tree, then backfill. Mound up the soil and create a furrow that directs water to the plant's roots. Gently firm down the soil, apply a handful of slow-release organic fertiliser, then water in thoroughly.

Be careful not to disturb the root structure as you plant, however if the tree is root-bound, you may need to untangle the roots and prune them.

Feeding and mulching

Lime trees are heavy feeders. Feed your lime tree at the beginning of spring and the end of summer with a high-nitrogen fertiliser. Mulch well with pea straw or lucerne hay to a depth of 10 cm beneath the canopy of the tree.

Watering

Limes love regular watering, but will not tolerate wet feet, hence the importance of good drainage. Water twice a week for the first two months while the plant is establishing, then cut back to once a week when the roots have set. Limes will appreciate extra watering when they are fruiting.

Pruning

In late winter or early spring, prune your tree to create a shape that is conducive to picking, not overcrowded with branches inside its canopy. If you are training your tree as an espalier, aim to create a full wall covering that soaks up heat and sunlight. Use a steel mesh grid for your trellising rather than wire lines.

Harvesting

Lime trees produce fruit twice a year. Falling fruit, fruit size and skin development are your best indicators that the fruit is ready. Hand-pick by twisting and pulling on developed fruit. The fruit keeps well on the tree.

MUSHROOM

Mushrooms are fungi disguised as a vegetable, which is not commonly grown by the home gardener, but it should be. While growing mushrooms at home will spoil the fun of a hunt, it will save you lengthy country expeditions to find vacant land to roam. Save those expeditions for when you may or may not be under the influence of its hallucinogenic cousin, and grow your edible mushrooms at home.

If you're wandering around old quarry sites in search of giant field mushrooms, as we did as kids, be careful when approaching what you may consider a 'dead set', 'absolute', 'for sure', 'first of the day!' mushroom, particularly if there is livestock nearby. Cow dung is the field mushroom's *doppelgänger*.

The greatest thing about growing mushrooms is that they won't steal any traditional growing space in your veggie patch, as they do not require sunlight. Instead, they need consistent temperature and moisture.

Botanical name
Various species

Family
Various, depending on the species

Little Veggie Patch favourite
Portobello

Companion plants
Mushrooms are grown by themselves, but you can use the exhausted compost to grow leafy greens.

How to grow
Mix spores with mushroom compost and place under cover

When to plant
>Zone 1: Any time
>Zone 2: Any time
>Zone 3: Any time
>Zone 4: Any time

Soil preparation
Use mushroom compost, which can be purchased from a nursery.

pH level
6.5–7.5

Position
Anywhere under cover, with consistent humidity/ temperature

Problems
Poor spawning

MUSHROOM

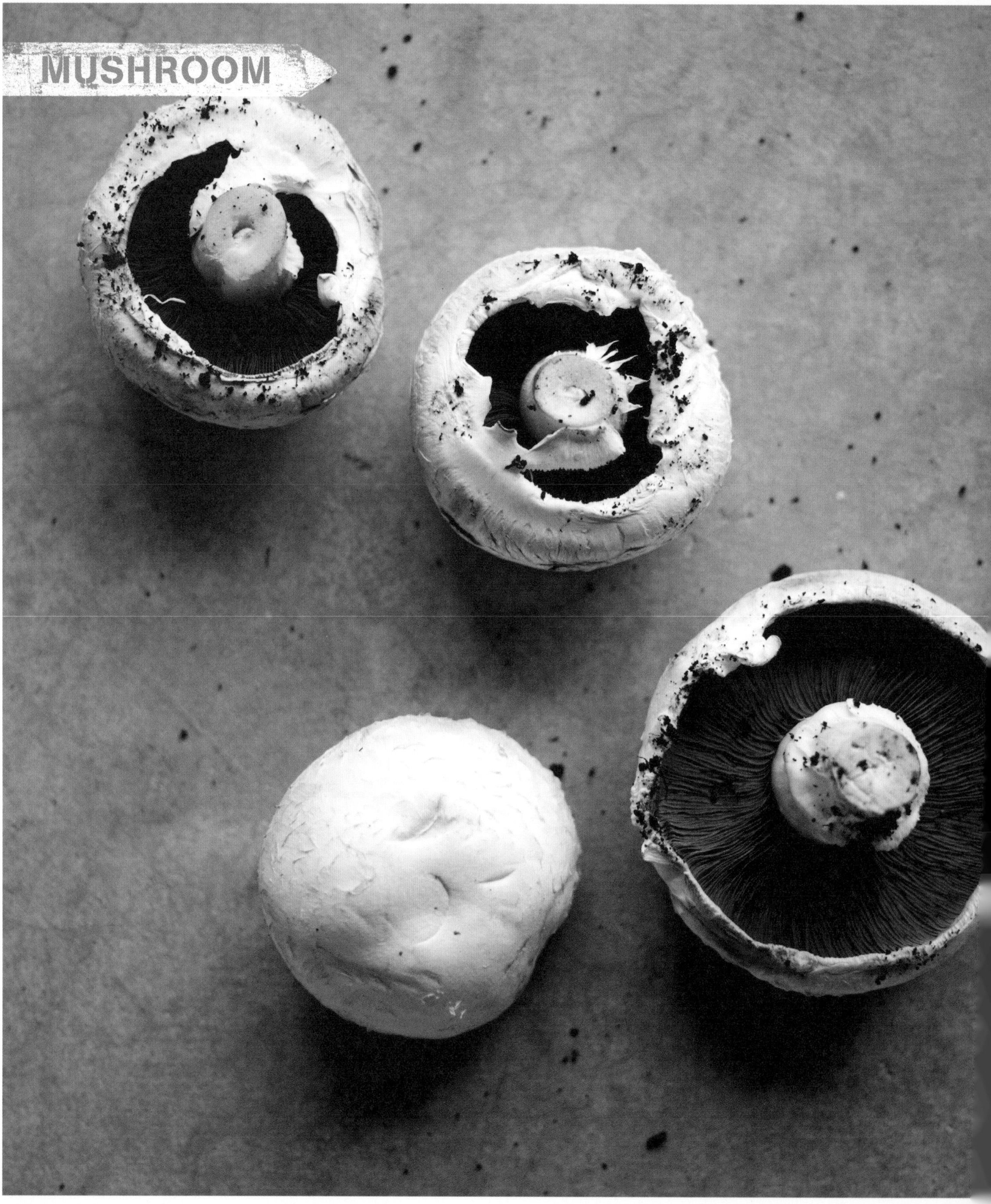

Place some mushroom compost in a heap outside, keeping it moist and turning it over for a couple of weeks. This will initiate decomposition. The amount of mushroom compost you will need will depend on the number and size of the the tubs you plan to grow your mushrooms in. Turn over the pile every 2–3 days, and after 2 weeks, place your compost (known as a 'substrate') in tubs and put them in an undercover spot that is cool and dark; the temperature and humidity should be consistent, so under the house is perfect.

At this stage the compost should have a sweet 'mushroom' smell to it and not the ammonium bite it featured when you first purchased it. If the composting process is incomplete, the mushrooms will be unlikely to grow.

After the tubs have settled in for a few days and found a consistent temperature, preferably somewhere around 25ºC, separate the mushroom spawn and mix it evenly through your compost, keeping the process sterile by wearing gloves.

Within a few days you will notice a white cottony growth appear, and after two weeks the mushroom will be in its full 'vegetative' state. At this point you will have nothing more than a thick layer of inedible, white cottony growth. As this process will have raised the temperature within your container, it is best to move them to a less humid spot for a day of ventilation.

Once they're back in their original space, the growth will need to be 'cased' for the edible mushrooms to form. The process of 'casing' essentially involves placing a layer of shredded paper, compost or straw on top of the growth. This casing, which should be 25–30 cm thick, activates the growth of the edible mushrooms. When applying the casing, make sure the material is soaking wet.

Within a few days you should notice the edible mushrooms developing.

It is vitally important to keep all your mushroom equipment as sterile as possible. Due to the nature of the growing conditions and also what you are growing, it is an ideal breeding ground for pests and diseases that can quickly take over. Make sure you adequately deal with any problem as soon as you encounter it.

Watering

After the initial process of decomposition, the material should be damp and not dried out when you place it in your tubs. Keeping them in a cool, dark position — for example, under the house — should prevent the compost from drying out.

If there is sufficient moisture as a result of the 'casing' process, you should not need to water the compost or casing material. But if you notice the contents drying out, give them a brief water — only enough to become damp again.

Harvesting

You can pick white mushrooms (*Agaricus bisporus*) at three stages of growth: button, cup and flat. As mushrooms mature, they open up and develop in appearance from button to flat. While becoming less dense, their flavour generally intensifies. Pick according to taste, texture and aesthetic.

When harvesting, pull upwards in a twisting motion, breaking each one off at the casing layer while removing as little of the casing material as possible. Brush off the casing and any compost from the mushroom, as it may cause discolouration.

You should get waves or 'flushes' of mushrooms growing for 2–4 weeks. When the flushes subside and only a few mushrooms are coming through, use the compost on your garden beds, particularly where you plan on growing leafy greens.

Growing in kits

Mushrooms can also be grown in kits, and by doing so you will save yourself from having to prepare the substrate and sort out your tubs.

Simply place the kit in an ideal location (somewhere cool and dark) and keep the ingredients watered, and within 1–2 weeks you will have flushes of mushrooms appearing. Flushes will last for 1–2 months.

Once the kits are exhausted, incorporate the casing material in your veggie beds as compost.

OLIVE

Olive trees are drought-resistant, hardy and largely disease- and pest-free. They are ideally suited to Australian conditions, particularly in the south, where many regions can replicate those of the Mediterranean, the source of a large portion of the world's olive production.

Evergreens with tough, silvery leaves, olive trees like hot summers, cool winters and little humidity. They can handle a variety of soil types but need good drainage, so ensure your chosen spot is well prepared with free-draining soil. If there is one thing olives don't like, it's wet feet.

The olive was the first tree to be cultivated; there are examples in Mediterranean Europe of trees that are up to 2000 years old. Their gnarled and twisted trunks and intricate root structure demonstrate this plant's staggering ability to use small amounts of water to survive.

While olives are a must on any self-respecting antipasto plate, olive oil is by far the fruit's most valuable by-product. The biggest producers of olive oil are in Spain, Italy and Greece, but Australian olive oil is building a reputation that can match Mediterranean quality, if not quantity.

If you plan on making your own olive oil at home, you will need to set yourself up with the correct infrastructure, which is expensive, or be prepared to deal with a 1:50 yield to effort ratio.

Botanical name
Olea europaea

Family
Oleaceae (Olive family)

Origin
Mediterranean

Little Veggie Patch favourite
Manzanillo

Space needs
Can be grown in larger pots but prefers being in-ground

Companion plants
Pretty happy by itself

How to grow
Transplant a bagged or potted adolescent tree

Where to plant
Olive trees are comfortable in dry, hot regions with cool winters, and will thrive throughout much of southern Australia.

When to plant
> Zone 1: March–June
> Zone 2: March–June
> Zone 3: April–June
> Zone 4: April–June

Soil preparation
Olive trees tolerate salinity and drought, but do not like to be waterlogged. Prepare free draining soil, with added compost and fresh animal manure.

pH level
7.0–8.0

Position
Sunny position

Spacing
5 m

Problems
Generally pest- and disease-free

Alternatively, you may find a local business willing to convert your olive harvest into oil for you. Ten kilograms of olives will make approximately 1–2 litres of olive oil, so it is worthwhile combining forces with friends and family to make the process worthwhile. Make sure you pick the olives as close to processing time as possible, otherwise they will become acidic and affect your oil's flavour.

Dig a hole twice the width of the root ball and a little shallower than the root ball's height. Moisten the hole with 10 litres of water before positioning the plant and backfilling. As you backfill, firm the soil down and water in to help it settle. Create a mound and furrow on the surface that will aid drainage and direct water to the roots. Drive in two stakes, about 30 cm on either side of the trunk, and use soft twine to tie the trunk to the stakes and hold the plant perfectly upright.

Feeding and mulching

Once a year, after you have harvested and pruned your tree, fertilise it with well-rotted animal manure. To suppress weeds and retain moisture, mulch around the base of the tree with a 10 cm layer of pea straw or lucerne hay.

Watering

The most important thing is not to waterlog the soil. Water your young plant twice a week for the first couple of months, then shift to once a week until it is one year old. After the first year, your olive tree should be able to survive on rainfall alone.

Pruning

If you notice any suckers, cut them back.

Olives fruit mostly on new growth, so you'll need to prune once a year after harvesting. Pruning will encourage new shoots and ensure the tree won't become overcrowded. Aim to create four strong internal branches coming out at 45-degree angles. This will open up the canopy to admit light and allow airflow.

Harvesting

Olives fruit every year, but most prolifically every second. They take 6 months to ripen, and you will find that not all the fruit ripens at the same time. Harvest when most of the olives are turning brown. It can be a time-consuming process, as it is best to hand-pick. If harvesting for oil, lay a sheet at the base of your tree to catch the olives you dislodge with a soft rake.

Remember that ripe olives are not edible. They will need to be soaked and salted before you can eat them.

Nonna's Kitchen

Marinated olives

1–2 kg green olives

7–10 lemons

salt

2 sprigs fresh oregano, leaves roughly chopped

2–3 garlic cloves, thinly sliced

2–3 chillies, thinly sliced

good-quality extra virgin olive oil

> Harvest a large bowl full of green olives from the tree. Crush the olives with a back of the knife blade and remove the pips.

> Place olives in a large bowl, cover with water, add the juice of one lemon (this will stop the olives going dark) and a pinch of salt.

> Strain the water the next day, replacing with the same quantity of water, lemon juice and salt, and repeat this daily until the olives taste right – the longer you leave them the mellower the flavour will become. This should take somewhere between 7 and 10 days.

> Strain the olives and let them dry, then place them in a sterilised jar with the oregano, garlic and chilli, and cover with oil.

> Store in the fridge and eat over the coming weeks or months, depending on your appetite.

ONION

It is the gas of the onion that makes you cry, quite randomly, like your children. The gas is released as you chop through the onion and it reacts with the water in your tear ducts to create sulphuric acid. Rule of thumb — the older the onion, the stronger the gas created.

All that being said, goggle-wearing is frowned upon, and crying should be seen as a necessary pleasure versus pain trade-off for using this great culinary vegetable.

Most onion types, especially the traditional bulbing varieties, are most suited to cooler climates; however, the home gardener will find certain varieties that perform better in warmer climates. Multiple bulbing onions, such as French shallots and bunching onions (spring onions), do suit warmer conditions.

If you intend growing bulbing onions, be prepared for a lengthy growing period, as it will take 4–6 months before they're ready for harvest. For the home vegetable garden, where space is at a premium, multiple bulbing and bunching varieties are a better investment of your veggie-growing real estate.

Botanical name
Allium cepa

Family
Amaryllidaceae (Onion family)

Origin
Russia

Little Veggie Patch favourite
Red Dwarf

Space needs
Suited to larger pots, but prefer an in-ground veggie patch

Companion plant
Carrot

How to grow
Propagate in seed trays

When to plant
> Zone 1: February–September
> Zone 2: February–August
> Zone 3: February–July
> Zone 4: March–June

Soil preparation
The soil should be well-drained and not contain excessive nitrogen. The main requirement for onions is potassium, so apply wood ash or potash prior to planting.

pH level
6.5

Position
Full sun, in a spot that follows leafy green crops such as lettuce or cabbage.

Spacing
5–10 cm

Problems
Fungal diseases, poor germination

ONION

Sow seed in seed trays at a depth of 0.5–1.0 cm before covering and watering in. Transplant into the patch about a month after germination, or when the seedlings have developed to a point that makes handling possible. Seed varieties vary, depending on the time of season they are to be planted — early, mid- or late — so select a variety that suits your planting requirements.

Note: Ensure you source your onion seeds from a reputable organic seed supplier, as onions can suffer from poor germination.

Feeding and mulching

Be careful not to overfeed your onions with nitrogen, as too much will cause excessive growth of foliage at the expense of the bulb. When the seedlings have been in-ground for a month, mulch with pea straw or lucerne hay to a depth of 3–5 cm.

As they grow, mound soil around the stems, as onion bulbs have a habit of protruding from the ground.

Watering

As with garlic, water 2–3 times a week during the infancy and adolescent stages, then start to cut back to once a week for mature plants.

Harvesting

Onions are slow-growing and take up to 6 months to produce mature, fully bulbed roots. To accelerate the growth of the bulbs, tie a knot in the foliage once the plants are 4 months old. This apparently transfers growing energy from the leaf to the bulb.

Once the foliage begins to brown and die off, onions are ready to be harvested. Simply grab the stem growth and pull each onion out of the soil.

Mature onions can stay in the ground to dry out, but if wet weather is predicted, it is best to harvest them and store them in a cool, dry place.

ORANGE

An orange tree is for anyone sick of paying $5 for a small watered-down juice from the local café. Oranges are evergreen trees with dark green, glossy leaves and usually thin trunks and branches. There are a number of varieties that differ in size, the sweetness or sourness of the fruit and their ability to cope with differing climatic conditions.

Orange trees are easy to grow and can be prolific producers of fruit, yet on the domestic front they seem to be the ignored citrus. If you want to grow an orange tree, you need a hot, sunny spot with free-draining soil. Due to the size of their fruit, orange trees require more regular watering than any other variety. One of the great assets of citrus, apart from their bi-annual harvests, is the ability of the fruit to keep on the tree for long periods without rotting. Word on the street is that one of the great assets of the orange itself, is that when used in old-school police interrogation it leaves the suspect bruise-free.

While the orange is primarily used for its flesh and juice, the rind contains an oil that infuses and enhances dishes, making it a popular ingredient in cooking. That same oil is also a natural repellent of slugs and snails and can be used to fight these pests organically. To do so, simply scatter twisted orange rinds through the affected areas of your garden bed.

Botanical name
Citrus sinensis, C. aurantium

Family
Rutaceae (Citrus family)

Origin
China

Little Veggie Patch favourite
Blood (varieties of *Citrus sinensis*)

Space needs
Can be grown in larger pots but prefers being in-ground

Companion plants
Garlic, onion, nasturtium, lavender

How to grow
Transplant a bagged or potted adolescent tree

When to plant
>Zone 1: September–November
>Zone 2: September–November
>Zone 3: October–December
>Zone 4: October–December

Where to plant
Oranges enjoy a warm, humid climate with cool to mild winters.

Soil preparation
A fortnight before planting, prepare a free-draining, light soil that is integrated with compost and fresh animal manure.

pH level
5.5–6.5

Position
Sunny, sheltered position in free-draining soil

Spacing
3–4 m

Problems
Aphids

When comparing the citrus varieties, we look at it like this. A lemon tree will produce too much fruit, but is a must, so espalier them to contain the amount of fruit. Oranges will produce a lot of fruit that will be used, so concentrate your growing efforts on this tree and dedicate your largest space to it. And finally, lime, the great unknown, will potentially make you rich, so choose your best spot for this variety, then tell all your contacts at the bars and restaurants to hold tight, and cross your fingers.

When planting, dig a hole the width of the root ball but a little shallower than its height so you can mound the soil around the rest of the roots and ensure good drainage. Before positioning the plant, moisten the hole with about 10 litres of water so that it penetrates the surrounding soil. Position the tree, then backfill. Mound up the soil and create a furrow that directs water to the plant's roots. Gently firm down the soil, apply a handful of slow-release organic fertiliser and water in thoroughly.

Be careful not to disturb the root structure as you plant, however if the tree is root-bound, you may need to untangle the roots and prune them.

Drive a stake 30 cm on either side of the trunk (away from the roots) and use soft twine to brace the trunk upright between the two.

Clean away any fallen fruit to reduce susceptibility to pests and disease.

Feeding and mulching

Feed your orange tree with a high-nitrogen and -phosphorus fertiliser twice a year, at the end of winter and in summer. Water in well after doing so. Keep grass and weeds away from the root system by mulching with a 10 cm layer of pea straw or lucerne hay.

Watering

Water the plant twice a week in the first year, moreso during the first month while it is finding its feet, but be careful not to let the soil become waterlogged. Cut back to once a week thereafter. Increase watering when fruiting.

Pruning

Prune the tree to keep the canopy from becoming overcrowded and to facilitate harvesting. Cut back any low-lying branches that, when laden with fruit, may hang to the ground.

Harvesting

When the fruit starts to fall from the tree, you'll know it is ripe, but bear in mind that it will be ripe well before then, as oranges keep particularly well on the tree. Taste test the fruit for sweetness when it is a desirable size. Hand-pick by twisting and pulling.

SCARECROWS

One rule of scarecrow building is that if it can frighten the creator, it can surely frighten away birds and pests. An intimidating scarecrow with an awkwardly high centre of gravity, named Luigi, was added to Mat's vegetable garden last year. Luigi was incredibly lifelike, pieced together from Mat's old gardening clothes to the extent that it could sometimes be mistaken for him, or at least for someone who had just raided his wardrobe.

Because of Luigi's unusually high centre of gravity, any day the northerly picked up above 25 km/h, he would be left lying face down in the dirt. Whoever confronted this human-like silhouette face down in the vegetable garden would go pale until they realised it was only Luigi. The primal fear of stumbling across a lifeless body in his vegetable garden gripped Mat time and time again. However, Luigi face down in the dirt indicated to birds and other large pests that stress-free feeding on the vegetables was the go. Upright, Luigi was an imposing, riskier proposition.

A lot of people question the effectiveness of scarecrows in the veggie patch, as birds and other pests have evolved to understand that the mass of sticks and hay and old clothing standing in the vegetable garden isn't a real threat. It just means we have to evolve our building practices to make more effective scarecrows, which not only scare the sense out of you as the sideline show, but also make feeding on your veggies a nerve-racking and risky endeavour.

Scarecrow building is an imaginative and fun project. Create one that is a credible protector of your crops. You need to give your scarecrow stature and attitude.

Building a scarecow

There is no substitute or replacement for Luigi, may he rest in peace, so it is time to create a new protector of crops (AKA vegetable monster AKA heart stopper).

For this project you will need:

> old clothes
> gumboots
> 4 long wooden stakes
> thicker block of timber
  (about 0.5 m long)

> screws
> ball of string
> bale of straw
> hessian bag
> mask of choice (or buttons)

gin by constructing the frame of your arecrow. Attach two of the wooden stakes gether, making a crucifix shape – this will the arms and the upper body. Now grab ur thicker wooden block and screw the her two stakes to this to create the legs, th the sharp ends of the stakes as the feet.

Screw both segments together to make the completed frame. This should be quite sturdy, so use as many screws as you feel necessary. Trim off any excess length or unrequired sharp ends for safely.

Time to be the stylist here and clothe the scarecrow. Start by putting on the pants and filling them with straw to provide bulk and life. Then pierce the soles of the gum boots, forcing them over the pointy stakes and pulling them up until you can tuck in the pants.

nstruct the head and torso by stuffing a ssian bag with straw. Tie with string at e 'neck' and attach at this point to the nction of the crucifix.

Clothe the upper half of the scarecrow and attach a terrifying mask of your choice to the hessian bag or, alternatively, to avoid unnecessary panic among human kind, use any old buttons you may have in the sewing box to make the facial features.

Select a spot in the veggie patch for your creation and hammer in the legs. The sturdier the frame, the easier it is to drive the scarecrow into the ground. Otherwise you will have another Luigi episode on your hands!

PARSNIP

If there were a cross-breeding machine for vegetables, and someone was granted the opportunity to create a new vegetable variety by throwing in a carrot with a sweet potato, we'd be hitting them over the head with the largest parsnip we could find. The fact that the parsnip is actually related to the carrot would be the motivation for the first whack.

Parsnip is without doubt our favourite roasting vegetable. Its combination of taste and texture draws on the characteristics of potatoes, turnips, pumpkins and carrots.

It is best grown in cooler climates, as it relies on frost to develop the starch in the vegetable into sugar, giving it its sweet taste.

This vegetable really is a challenge for the home gardener. Poor germination and viability of the seed have made good seed sources difficult to come by. They also store badly, quickly becoming soft once harvested.

If you're the sort of person who would hang up your boots after scoring a hat trick in your first game of football, we encourage you to try this first up, and if you nail it, pack up and move onto something different.

Botanical name
Pastinaca sativa

Family
Apiaceae (Carrot family)

Origin
Mediterranean

Little Veggie Patch favourite
Melbourne White Skin

Space needs
Suited to smaller pots

Companion plants
Parsnip helps fruit trees by attracting beneficial insects with their strongly scented flowers.

How to grow
Sow seeds directly into the patch

When to plant
> Zone 1: August–February
> Zone 2: July–March
> Zone 3: February–September
> Zone 4: March–May

Soil preparation
Parsnips prefer a deep, friable soil type that is not overly rich with nitrogen. Use compost to break up the soil, allowing easier passage for the roots.

They will require high levels of potassium, so apply potash.

pH level
6.5–7.0

Position
Full sun, but will tolerate shade, so this is a good opportunity to use the 'B grade' zone of your patch. Plant where leafy greens were growing the previous season.

Spacing
10–15 cm

Problems
Root rot, splitting roots

This vegetable needs some frost to develop its flavour, so those living in cool-climate zones are in luck. Soak seeds in water overnight before planting, then sow directly into the patch at a depth of 0.5–1 cm, backfill and water in. Keep the seeds moist during the germination period; covering them with a damp hessian bag can help to lock in the moisture. Once they have germinated, thin them out.

Feeding and mulching

Mulch with a 3–5 cm layer of pea straw or lucerne hay. A mid-season application of compost and potash will meet their feeding requirements.

Watering

Water 2–3 times a week for the first month. Thereafter keep the watering consistent and don't overwater. Too much water will rot the root, while insufficient watering will cause the root to split. The idea is to keep the soil moist without making it wet, so your watering plan will need to consider rainfall and heat.

Harvesting

Once the foliage has started to die back, use a garden fork to remove the parsnips from the soil without breaking the root. If conditions are cool and not too wet, it is best to leave mature parsnips you can't use immediately in the ground, as they tend to store poorly once picked.

PASSIONFRUIT

A passionfruit is a hardy, vigorous evergreen vine that can provide a handsome cover for a wall or arch. This great climber will attach itself to any hold with ease, and quickly mature into a lush canopy of green, producing food within 18 months.

Native to South America, passionfruit enjoys heat and humidity. It is a hungry feeder that will thrive in well-drained soil with regular, thorough watering. Keep your vine well-pruned, encouraging growth that fits the shape and direction you desire. We often come across out-of-control vines that easily overwhelm trees, fences and sometimes homes, so staying on top of your plant is important.

Passionfruit vines produce fruit twice a year, with the sweetness of the fruit aided by regular watering and being left to ripen on the vine. Overfertilising with nitrogen will result in excessive foliage growth over fruit, so keep that in check and make sure you prune the vine each year to encourage new growth, from which the flowers and fruit grow.

Passionfruit requires bees to cross-pollinate the flowers, so make the area around your vine as sexy as possible. Planting lavender nearby will add to its appeal.

Botanical name
Passiflora edulus, *P. edulus* var. *flavicarpa*

Family
Passifloraceae (Passionfruit family)

Origin
South America

Little Veggie Patch favourite
Ned Kelly

Space needs
Suited to larger pots, but prefers an in-ground veggie patch

Companion plant
Marigold

How to grow
Transplant a bagged or potted adolescent plant

Where to plant
Australia-wide — there are varieties suitable for different conditions.

When to plant
>Zone 1: September–December
>Zone 2: September–November
>Zone 3: September–November
>Zone 4: August–October

Soil preparation
Will tolerate most soil types, but must be free-draining. Before planting, mix through compost and well-rotted animal manure.

pH level
6.5–7.5

Position
Full sun, away from other trees, on a trellis structure

Spacing
3–4 m

Problem
Aphids

Dig a hole twice as big and the same depth as the root ball, and backfill with soil to which you've added compost. Once you've planted your passionfruit, be careful not to disturb the roots. Firm down gently and water in thoroughly with liquid seaweed fertiliser. If the lead tendril is long enough, attach it to the trellis so that it stays upright, otherwise tie it to a small stake in the interim.

Feeding and mulching

As passionfruit is a heavy feeder, give it a good dose of an all-round fertiliser in the first year, before it begins to flower. Mulch to reduce competition from weeds and lock in moisture. It is best to use pea straw or lucerne hay to a depth of 10 cm.

Fertilise the vine with well-rotted chicken manure twice a year, at the beginning of spring and the beginning of autumn. Water in well after each application.

Also apply some potash when flowers appear.

Watering

Water 2–3 times a week for the first month, then cut back to one good soaking a week. Premature shrivelling of the passionfruit occurs when the plant has insufficient water to develop fruit, so keep the vine well-watered during flowering and fruiting.

Pruning

Watch out for suckers stealing energy from the main stem; these should be cut or pulled out at ground level. Staying on top of pruning is the most important element of growing passionfruit, as they are prolific creepers.

Fruit forms on the young growth, so in early spring cut back older, woody growth to keep the vine productive.

Harvesting

When the fruit starts to shrivel, twist and pull it from the vine. Regular picking and thorough watering during fruiting will result in an almost constant supply of fruit.

PEAS

Peas, like beans, are a great nitrogen-fixer that can be used as part of your crop rotation or integrated as green manure. Most of the plant, especially its young pods, is edible and tasty, so developing a full harvest of mature peas is probably unlikely.

If you, like us, have trouble growing enough peas to make even a snack, buy a bag of peas from the markets and practise your shelling technique. While doing so, recall Tony Greig describing Mark Waugh's slips catching in the 1990s — 'Just like shelling peas' — and somewhere along the way, you'll get your lines crossed like us and treat pea shelling as some sort of competitive sport. Soft thumbs and sharp nails are two key components of nonchalant shelling.

Peas are a cool-climate crop that is generally grown in autumn; however, there are varieties that will grow all year round in some climates. In Melbourne it is not unusual for the seeds contained in pea straw to germinate and mature until harvest during summer.

Botanical name
Pisum sativum var. *hortense*

Family
Fabaceae (Legume family)

Origin
Mediterranean

Little Veggie Patch favourite
Sugar Bon

Space needs
Suited to larger pots, but prefer an in-ground veggie patch

Companion plants
Beetroot, potato

How to grow
Sow directly into your patch

When to plant
> Zone 1: March–October
> Zone 2: March–September
> Zone 3: April–July
> Zone 4: Can't be grown in this region

Soil preparation
Prior to planting, prepare the soil with chook manure and ensure it is free-draining. Peas will also benefit from a small application of lime. Allow to settle for a week before planting.

pH level
6.5–7.5

Position
Full sun, up against a fence or trellis. Plant where you have previously grown, or are intending to grow, tomatoes, eggplants or capsicum (all members of the Solanaceae family).

Spacing
5–10 cm

Problems
Rodents, powdery mildew

Use a chopstick or pencil to form holes 3–5 cm deep, then place 2 seeds in each hole, cover, pat down and water in. If more than one seed germinates in a single hole, you will need to thin them out.

Build a good-sized trellis structure up against a fence or in the patch to allow room for the plant to grow. Regularly attach the pea growth to the trellis to stop it falling over under its own weight — a messy, congested pea plant sprawling along the ground will be more susceptible to pests and diseases.

Cutting back the tips will result in more branching and increased production.

Feeding and mulching

Peas provide their own nitrogen, so excessive nitrogen will result in prolific plant growth at the expense of the pods. Just before flowering, apply liquid potash to help the fruit to set. Mulch the ground with pea straw or lucerne hay to a depth of 3–5 cm to lock in moisture and prevent any stray branches from making contact with the soil.

Watering

Be careful not to water excessively before germination, as this may rot the seeds and make them more susceptible to rodent attack. Once the seeds have germinated, water 2–3 times a week for the first month, then cut back to once a week.

Harvesting

The entire plant is edible, from the plant shoots to the pods and the peas within. Pick pods by hand when they are at a desirable size. Smaller pods are sweeter and incredible eaten fresh. Picking pods will encourage others to develop.

POTATO

Prolific and versatile, the potato is one of the most consumed vegetables on planet earth and a staple in our diets. Unfortunately, most of the potatoes consumed in Australia take the form of either an oil-drenched hot chip or an equally oil-drenched and then dried crisp... Yeah, we know, yum...

Potatoes will always be remembered as a protagonist of The Little Veggie Patch Co. In pre-LVPC days, while preparing formal garden beds and lawns for an old employer, we began unearthing dozens and dozens of small, firm potatoes in what must have been an old veggie patch — unbeknownst to the owner. Once our fellow employees were alerted to this incredible find, we became preoccupied with the unique outcome of not only providing ourselves with an income that day but also the crux of a decent meal. A coup quickly followed, whereby work was refused without the potential of gaining a fresh meal in the process, and so our landscaping days were quickly over.

Growing potatoes is a fun activity for kids, who can build and harvest a spud tower that is as close to a 'sure thing' treasure hunt as you can have in a vegetable patch (see page 168).

Potatoes are best suited to cooler and temperate climates, so the propagation times depend on where you live.

Botanical name
Solanum tuberosum

Family
Solanaceae (Nightshade family)

Origin
South America

Little Veggie Patch favourite
Nicola

Space needs
Suited to larger pots, but prefer an in-ground veggie patch

Companion plants
Horseradish, bean

How to grow
Sow sprouting tubers

When to plant
> Zone 1: September–January
> Zone 2: August–October
> Zone 3: August–October
> Zone 4: April–May
   + September–October
   + December–January

Soil preparation
Prepare a friable, well-drained, compost-rich soil

pH level
5.0–6.0

Position
Will tolerate part shade. For ease of harvest and better use of space, best grown in a spud tower (see page 168).

Spacing
30 cm

Potatoes prefer mild conditions — anywhere between 16° and 22°C is an ideal temperature. It is common to grow potatoes directly into a mix of fresh compost, well-rotted animal manure and straw. No-dig gardens are ideal, as they will drain perfectly. Sow the sprouting tubers directly into the mix of compost, straw and well-rotted manure at a depth of approximately 15 cm. Water prior to planting and also water in well afterwards.

If planting in the patch, avoid planting where potatoes or tomatoes have previously been grown in the last couple of seasons.

Feeding and mulching

If growing your spuds in a no-dig garden (see page 19), the decomposition of the contents will help feed the plants over their lifetime. Otherwise a fortnightly application of a liquid seaweed fertiliser will suffice.

When building a spud tower, allow the first shoots to mature to a height of 20–30 cm before covering them with a fresh mix of well-wetted compost and straw. Repeat this process to create 3 levels in your spud tower.

When growing potatoes in the ground, build up the soil around the bases of the plants to avoid exposing the developing tubers to sunlight. Mulching the ground is also highly recommended. Do so with a 5–10 cm layer of pea straw or lucerne hay.

Watering

Water well. Once or twice a week, over the lifetime of the plants, is ideal.

Harvesting

When the plants start to die back, about 4 months after planting, the spuds are mature and ready for picking. Small, sweet and crisp potatoes can be harvested any time after 2–3 months.

If you have created a spud tower, the harvesting process is easy and fun. Carefully dismantle your tower, thus allowing the contents to spill out. Forage through the contents for your spuds.

If you are harvesting out of a patch, gently fork the soil surrounding the potato plants and then fumble through the soil for dislodged spuds.

Potatoes store well in the ground except when conditions are wet or overly warm.

PUMPKIN

Pumpkin is a large investment in every sense of the word. The plant itself is a vigorous grower that can be either trellised or allowed to crawl over the ground. The fruit usually takes 4 or more months to mature and can reach weights in excess of 500 kg.

While the main prize is the fruit itself, most of the pumpkin plant — shoots, flowers, leaves and seeds — is edible. In fact, one summery afternoon a Zambian lady passed our front-yard jungle of pumpkin vines, and asked if she could pinch a few leaves for a meal she was preparing. We happily swapped some leaves for the recipe.

If you choose to trellis your pumpkin vine, spend some time shoring up the structure. If you leave it to sprawl across the ground, keep it away from your other veggie-growing activities, as it will bully your other plants for space.

Pumpkins are very frost-sensitive and should be propagated after the last frost of spring, and harvested before the first of autumn.

If you have a hankering to make a jack 'o' lantern for Halloween, opt for the larger and scarier 'Atlantic Giant' variety. If you want to take up a competitive sport, pumpkin throwing is huge these days.

Botanical name
Cucurbita maxima

Family
Cucurbitaceae

Origin
Central and South America

Little Veggie Patch favourite
Jack Be Strong

Space needs
Best grown in an in-ground veggie patch

Companion plant
Sweetcorn

How to grow
Sow seed directly into the patch

When to plant
> Zone 1: October–December
> Zone 2: September–December
> Zone 3: August–February
> Zone 4: February–September

Soil preparation
Your soil should be free-draining and moderately fertile, so add compost before planting. It will tolerate a number of soil types.

pH level
6.5–7.0

Position
Full sun with plenty of room to move. Position on the edge of your growing space, allowing it to creep *away* from your growing space, or set up a solid trellis structure on which to grow it vertically.

Spacing
1.5 m

Problems
Powdery mildew

The best technique is to sow the seed, 2–3 cm deep, directly into small mounds of compost. This will ensure adequate nutrition and drainage. Keep well watered until the seeds germinate. Although pumpkin is the most frost-tolerant of the cucurbits, it is best to plant it when conditions are regularly above 18°C. If you are growing your pumpkin at ground level, peg down the vine at intervals to avoid wind damage. If you are training your pumpkin, regularly attach the vines to the structure as it matures. To encourage the plant to branch out, which will improve its size and the amount of produce, pinch out the growth tips, which will cause it to fork.

Pumpkin has problems with pollination, so you may need to hand-pollinate to increase the likelihood of fruit setting. When the female flowers open, pick a number of mature male flowers (rub your finger in the flower to see if pollen comes off) and rub the male flowers inside the female ones.

The female flower, which you will find attached close to the main stem, will have a tiny pumpkin in between the flower and stem. The male flowers, prevalent in larger numbers than the female flowers, don't have the tiny pumpkin, and can be located further off the vine. The stem of the male flower is thinner.

Feeding and mulching

To satisfy its nutrient demands, apply a liquid seaweed fertiliser once a fortnight. If growing your pumpkin at ground level, mulch well around where the plant will grow to avoid the risk of disease and fruit rot. Apply pea straw or lucerne hay to a depth of 3–5 cm.

Harvesting

Use a knife to cut the pumpkin from the vine about 5 cm below the stem. If you cut too close to the stem, you will jeopardise the storing ability of the fruit. Pumpkins store better if allowed to dry in the sun for up to 3 days after harvest. Part of this process will occur on the vine, where the pumpkin will also develop its flavour.

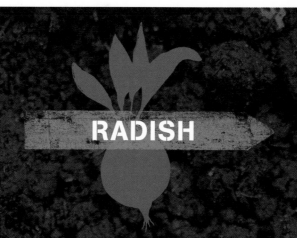

RADISH

Radishes are the ideal first vegetable to grow, as only people with the black thumbs of death would be unable to grow them.

Growing radishes is the perfect introduction for your kids, too, as the growing process occurs in rapid succession — the seeds germinate within a couple days of sowing, and you can harvest after only 4 weeks. Radishes can be grown across a wide range of climates (all year in many cases), and are able to tolerate various soil types.

All varieties of radish are relatively pest- and disease-free, and if left to flower, will attract beneficial predators, including native bees and parasitic wasps.

The flavour of the root tends to develop with time, so those left to mature will generally be spicier. Consistent watering will help ensure the roots are solid and not split at harvest time.

Botanical name
Raphanus sativus

Family
Brassicaceae (Mustard family)

Origin
Asia and Europe

Little Veggie Patch favourite
Cherry Belle

Space needs
Suited to smaller pots

Companion plants
Carrot, lettuce

How to grow
Sow directly into your patch

When to plant
>Zone 1: Any time
>Zone 2: Any time
>Zone 3: Any time
>Zone 4: Any time

Soil preparation
Radishes will grow in most soil types, but prefer a free-draining, friable soil to allow room for easy root growth. Add compost a week prior to planting.

pH level
6.5–7.5

Position
Full sun, part shade

Spacing
5 cm

Problems
Snails and slugs

Choose a variety that suits your climatic conditions and sow directly into the patch. Create a shallow trench with your finger to a depth of 0.5–1 cm, then sprinkle the seeds evenly along the trench line and backfill. Otherwise sprinkling the seed and gently brushing over a thin layer of soil will suffice. Water in with an application of liquid seaweed fertiliser.

Radishes are fast-growing, so it is possible to get your first harvest as you thin out the seedlings.

Feeding and mulching

Excessive nitrogen will result in prolific leaf growth at the expensive of root growth, so don't overfertilise. A fortnightly application of liquid seaweed fertiliser will suffice. Mulch the soil with pea straw or lucerne hay to a depth of 3–5 cm.

Watering

Your radishes will appreciate regular watering to ensure the roots do not split. Water them 2–3 times a week over their lifetime.

Harvesting

Pull out smaller radishes by their leaf growth, and use a garden fork to carefully loosen the soil before harvesting the larger ones, otherwise you may snap them along the root.

You can also harvest the leaf growth for salads. Avoid picking too many leaves from the one plant, as it may affect root development.

SPUD TOWERS

It's always a pleasant surprise to come across a garden with undiscovered treasure lying just below the surface. While potatoes are easy to grow, it is an activity best suited to a purpose-built unit, known as a spud tower, so that your other veggies go undisturbed while you're harvesting. It also facilitates an easy and fun harvesting process for your kids.

Spud towers are simple to construct and require only a few materials. The idea is that as the potatoes grow and send up leaf growth, this growth is then covered with compost, which forces the plant to send out more roots and therefore more potatoes. As you keep repeating this process, your spud tower grows and grows, filling up with new tubers and more bounty. The process comes to a head when it is ultimately time to destroy and harvest your tower and seek out the potato treasure.

Building a spud tower

Spud towers are easy to assemble and can be created anywhere in your garden – even on a patch of grass.

For this activity you'll need:

> 2 × 1.2 m wooden stakes

> 2 m chicken mesh wire

> twine or thin wire

> bale of straw

> 2 × 40-litre bags of compost

> 3 sprouting potatoes

1

Pick a suitable location (can be in the bed or on the grass) and drive two wooden stakes into the earth about 50 cm apart. Using the stakes as a frame, construct a circular enclosure of chicken mesh wire, strengthening your structure with twine or thin wire.

2

Leaving the centre hollow, line your inner walls with straw to a height of 30 cm.

3

Fill the centre with compost.

Place your sprouting potatoes in the compost to a depth of 3–5 cm.

5

Water in the potatoes.

When the spud growth is about 30 cm high, line walls with another layer of straw, 30 cm deep, and cover the plant growth with compost. Repeat the process once more (or until your spud tower is full). When the top plant growth of your final level starts to die back, it is time to hunt for spud treasure.

ROCKET

The ultimate grazing green, rocket or arugula is a spicy, peppery lettuce. In Italy it is used in everything from salads to pizza and pasta, as well as in some cheeses. It has a distinctive flavour that scents your fingertips when you harvest it. Altogether a beautiful thing.

'My father, born and bred in Kalgoorlie, Western Australia, who married an Italian woman and so now considers himself European and sophisticated, regards rocket as "a vegetable important to our identity as Italians".' – MP

Like most leafy greens, it is easy to grow and will tolerate part shade. Rocket thrives in cooler weather but has a tendency to bolt to seed in warmer conditions.

Rocket and shaved parmesan cheese with balsamic vinegar dressing make the ideal light summer salad to complement a heavy afternoon pasta.

Botanical name
Eruca sativa

Family
Brassicaceae (Mustard family)

Origin
Mediterranean and Asia

Little Veggie Patch favourite
Astro

Space needs
Suited to smaller pots

Companion plants
Carrot, radish

How to grow
Sow seed directly into the patch

When to plant
>Zone 1: Any time
>Zone 2: Any time
>Zone 3: Any time
>Zone 4: Any time

Soil preparation
Incorporate compost and well-rotted manure into the soil a week prior to planting.

pH level
6.5–7.0

Position
Full sun, part shade. Don't grow where you have previously grown brassica crops.

Spacing
15 cm

Sow seed at a depth of approximately 0.5–1.0 cm, then backfill with soil and water in. Rocket grows better in cool conditions, so either plant when temperatures are suitable or choose a heat-tolerant variety. Letting rocket go to seed will result in some self-seeding plants that will germinate when conditions are ideal.

If the plant starts to go to seed, pick off the seed heads as they appear. This should transfer growth back to the leaf.

Feeding and mulching

Apply a liquid seaweed fertiliser fortnightly, and mulch with either pea straw or lucerne hay to a depth of 3–5 cm.

Watering

Young rocket seedlings need watering 2–3 times a week until they are ready to pick. After you start harvesting, keep the soil well-watered so it does not completely dry out.

Harvesting

Pick leaf by leaf from 4 weeks after germination onwards. Harvesting will help generate further growth and prevent the plant going to seed. Its lovely spicy flavour intensifies with age.

SILVERBEET

Silverbeet is easy to grow, particularly hardy and looks absolutely brilliant as rainbow chard, but then mysteriously runs out of positive attributes just as it hits the kitchen table. 'Versatile' is one word people use to describe its culinary uses, but that is just another way of saying 'lacking a strong personality'.

If you grew up in an Italian family, chances are your Nonna would boil silverbeet in salty water, mixed through with olive oil and garlic, alright the first 46 times you had it. Try challenging her to prepare it in any other way and she would retaliate with a look that silenced you. The test for the home gardener is not to grow healthy, plentiful, beautiful-looking silverbeet, rather to conjure a dish that it absolutely owns and dictates.

When it comes to spring onions, we harp on about home veggie gardening being about growing vegetables that are more accessible substitutes, so some honesty is needed in saying that there is some resentment towards silverbeet. This should not stop you growing it, of course, as it is a more tolerant and prolific version of spinach, and if there is one vegetable you won't be able to kill, no matter how hard you may try, it is silverbeet.

Botanical name
Beta vulgaris cicla

Family
Chenopodiacea (Beet family)

Origin
Asia, Europe and North Africa

Little Veggie Patch favourite
Five Colours Rainbow

Space needs
Suited to smaller pots

Companion plants
Herbs, onion, beetroot

How to grow
Sow seed directly into the patch

When to plant
>Zone 1: September–March
>Zone 2: August–May
>Zone 3: Any time
>Zone 4: February–September

Soil preparation
Prepare your soil with fresh manure and compost a fortnight before planting. Integrate organic matter to increase its water-holding ability.

pH level
6.5–7.0

Position
Full sun, but will benefit from shading in warm weather, so plant next to larger plants, such as sweetcorn, or around onions and beetroot.

Spacing
30–40 cm

Problems
Snails and slugs

If, for whatever reason, you too decide that silverbeet is crap and want to move onto bigger and better things, try carrots — they do especially well where silverbeet has previously grown.

Silverbeet will boost your growing confidence. Soak seeds in water overnight prior to planting, then sow directly into your patch at a depth of about 0.5–1.0 cm. Backfill, then water in with an application of liquid seaweed fertiliser. Thin out once they have germinated, which should take about 2 weeks. Similar to spinach, silverbeet seeds produce multiple shoots that can be left in those clusters.

Feeding and mulching

As it's a large leafy green, silverbeet will appreciate regular applications of liquid seaweed fertiliser once a fortnight. Mulch the ground with pea straw or lucerne hay.

Watering

Keep well watered initially, approximately 2–3 times a week for the first month. Thereafter cut back to once a week, or according to the weather conditions.

Harvesting

Silverbeet is another grazing green — simply snap off the outer leaves as you need them. You can pick silverbeet from 6 weeks onwards over a lengthy harvesting period. Picking leaves will discourage the plant from bolting to seed and prevent the leaves from turning bitter.

SPINACH

Popeye, that strange-looking, tattooed, indecipherable, ill-mannered sailor was not only a comic success but also the undisputed champion of spinach. Without doubt the best part of the cartoon series was the moment Popeye would scoff a tin of spinach and transform into a strange-looking, tattooed, indecipherable, ill-mannered sailor with bulging biceps. It has since become common knowledge that spinach is a high source of iron; however it is unlikely to turn you into a bicep-swinging, goggle-eyed man of the sea.

Spinach is also rich in just about every good vitamin and mineral known to man, but like all living things, its nutritional value will start to diminish a couple of days after harvest.

Spinach is an annual plant best grown in cooler climates. There are varieties that will suit warmer conditions, but it generally tends to bolt to seed when stressed by warmer weather. Perpetual varieties can be left in the ground and harvested over a number of seasons. The best way to harvest spinach, like many lettuces, is to graze leaf by leaf, thereby promoting new and continual growth.

Botanical name
Spinacia oleracea

Family
Chenopodiaceae (Beet family)

Origin
Iran

Little Veggie Patch favourite
Bloomsdale

Space needs
Suited to smaller pots

Companion plant
Strawberry

How to grow
Sow seed directly into the patch

When to plant
> Zone 1: April–October
> Zone 2: March–September
> Zone 3: April–June
> Zone 4: Can't be grown in
       this region

Soil preparation
Prepare the beds by digging through compost and well-rotted manure a week prior to planting. Make sure the soil drains well.

pH level
6.0–7.0

Position
Full sun, part shade. Does not tolerate hot conditions. Plant next to your strawberries, as they tend to work well as companions.

Spacing
20 cm

Problems
Tendency to bolt to seed, magnesium deficiency

Sow seed into the patch at a depth of 0.5–1 cm, then backfill with soil and water in. Soaking the seed in water overnight before planting will help with germination. Make sure the temperature is sufficiently cool — it should be in the range of 10–15°C.

Two to three plants will germinate from each seed, and it is best to leave these clusters together.

Feeding and mulching

After planting, mulch the ground with a nutrient-rich mulch such as pea straw or lucerne hay to a depth of 3–5 cm. This will help lock in moisture and keep the soil temperature cool. Spinach will need fortnightly feedings of liquid seaweed fertiliser. If the plant receives insufficient nutrient and minerals, the leaves will start to yellow or the growth will be stunted.

Harvesting

Spinach is a grazing green, so gently hand-pick or cut the outside leaves of the plant when they are large enough. The root system of the plant is rather shallow, so be careful when picking not to disturb or pull at them. Picking leaves will encourage further production and regulate the plant's attempt to go to seed.

SPRING ONION

Spring onions are one of the easiest vegetables to grow. Space-smart and almost pest-free, these prolific growers have a milder taste than their onion counterparts, and are a versatile ingredient in an array of dishes.

One of the best ways to go about home veggie gardening is to find substitutes for some vegetables that can be either difficult or time-consuming to grow. Spring onions are a far more accessible alternative to the common onion. Stagger your planting to enjoy an almost constant supply of spring onions in the veggie patch.

If you buy a bunch from the markets and find you have more than necessary — almost every time without fail — plant the remainder in the garden and keep them in the ground until you need them.

Pretty much the only thing about vegetables that slightly churns our stomachs is the gooey slime that builds up within the green shoots of spring onions. In our experience, the more mature the onion, the greater its propensity to contain the slime. While it is completely harmless, try to harvest your spring onions young, as a lot of people can find this a little off-putting, especially in salads.

Botanical name
Allium fistulosum

Family
Amaryllidaceae (Onion family)

Origin
Russia

Little Veggie Patch favourite
Pompei

Space needs
Suited to smaller pots

Companion plants
Lettuce, chamomile, beetroot, tomato

How to grow
Sow seed directly into the patch or propagate in seed trays

When to plant
>Zone 1: Any time
>Zone 2: Any time
>Zone 3: Any time
>Zone 4: Any time

Soil preparation
Spring onions will tolerate most soil types, but will grow more freely in friable, well-worked, free-draining earth. Prepare your soil with compost

and well-rotted manure a week prior to planting.

pH level
6.0–7.0

Position
Full sun, will tolerate some shade. Plant among your lettuces to create a salad grazing area.

Spacing
2–5 cm

Problems
Relatively pest- and disease-free

Sow seed at a depth of 0.5–1 cm, or propagate in seed trays and transplant. Spring onions don't mind being transplanted, and find their feet quickly. To transplant, dig a shallow trench, approximately 2 cm deep and 4 cm wide, and lay the seedlings down at intervals of 2–3 cm, with the roots sitting in the trench line. Backfill over the root, firming down gently and watering in with liquid seaweed fertiliser. Over a day or two the shoots will stand up in search of sunlight. Stagger planting times to ensure a regular and constant harvest.

Feeding and mulching

Apply liquid fertiliser every fortnight. Mulch well around the base of the plants once they have been in the ground for 2–3 weeks, otherwise it will be tough to avoid damaging them. Apply a 3–5 cm layer of pea straw or lucerne hay.

Watering

Spring onions require regular watering when young, about 3 times a week, but cut back to once a week when they are established.

Harvesting

Spring onions can be harvested at any size. The smaller plants are devoid of slime, one advantage of harvesting them when young. The plants can stay in the ground to mature without losing too much flavour.

Either pull out the entire plant by hand, or cut the stem of the plant to encourage new shoots to regenerate.

SQUASH

A relative of pumpkin and zucchini, squash is a warm-climate vegetable that is harvested as either a summer or winter variety. Summer squash is harvested early when the vegetable is about the size of a tennis ball, and tender, with a soft skin, like a zucchini. Winter squash is planted at the same time but is left to develop into a larger fruit with a hard skin, resembling that of a pumpkin.

You can encourage your squash plants to grow vertically or leave them to sprawl along the ground. Make sure the spot is well-drained and sunny. Varieties that grow as a bush rather than a creeper will require considerable space to mature, so choose their position wisely. If you choose to grow your plant vertically, set up a sturdy trellis structure to accommodate the weight of the fruit. Despite their weight, the fruits are not likely to drop off the plant and cause untold injury to your worst enemy.

Botanical name
Cucurbita pepo

Family
Cucurbitaceae (Gourd family)

Origin
South and Central America

Little Veggie Patch favourite
Sweet Dumpling

Space needs
Best grown in an in-ground veggie patch

Companion plants
Corn, nasturtium

How to grow
Propagate in individual seed cells

When to plant
>Zone 1: October–December
>Zone 2: September–December
>Zone 3: August–March
>Zone 4: February–September

Soil preparation
Indifferent to a number of soil types but must be free-draining. Mix through well-rotted manure a week prior to planting.

pH level
6.5–7.0

Position
Likes full sun and plenty of room

Spacing
1–1.5 m

Problems
Powdery mildew, poor germination in cold conditions

SQUASH

Sow seed into individual seed cells, at a depth 2–3 times the diameter of the seed, then backfill and water in. Keep indoors at night. Transplant, disturbing the root growth as little as possible. Squash don't like cooler temperatures, so the transplanting time will depend on the conditions at hand.

If you are growing a creeping variety, attach the plant to the trellis as it grows and pinch out the growth tips to encourage the plant to branch out.

Feeding and mulching

When transplanting, plant into a mound of compost; there will be little more nutrient demand from the plant. Mulch the ground thoroughly to prevent the fruit from making contact with the soil. Use pea straw or lucerne hay to create a layer 3–5 cm deep.

Watering

Water 2–3 times a week until the plant has become established. The compost will help the water to drain. After about a month, cut back to once a week then once the plant starts to produce fruit, increase the watering slightly.

Harvesting

Pick summer squash when they are young to encourage further production, as the plant can only hold a certain number of fruit at the one time. Alternatively, you can leave the fruit on the plant to become winter squash. To avoid damaging the plant while harvesting, cut off each fruit with a knife.

STRAWBERRY

Strawberry plants are perennial, which means they will produce fruit over a number of growing seasons. Like any perennial, however, their yield will peak and then start to decline after a few growing seasons, so it's advisable to replant the crop every 3 years.

Growing strawberries can be aided by any member of the onion (allium) family, so it's a good idea to engage in companion planting to enhance your success. Grow your spring onions in between strawberries and both will grow fantastically well.

If, like us, you had a rebellious childhood, picking strawberries from the veggie patch was about as naughty as you would get. We were never allowed to eat many of them, and as they tasted better than sugared lollies they became a highly sought-after treat. As kids we found it best to pick strawberries while the adults were talking about politics or religion.

Botanical name
Fragaria hybrida

Family
Rosaceae (Rose family)

Origin
South America

Little Veggie Patch favourite
Temptation

Space needs
Suited to smaller pots

Companion plants
All members of the onion family

How to grow
Plant as seedlings, or as runners from other plants.

When to plant
>Zone 1: Any time
>Zone 2: Any time
>Zone 3: Any time
>Zone 4: Any time

Soil preparation
Dig through compost and fresh manure a fortnight before planting.

pH level
5.0–6.0

Position
Full sun with good airflow and well-drained soil. Avoid planting in a spot that has previously grown tomatoes.

Spacing
30 cm

Problems
Birds, snails and slugs, ants

STRAWBERRY

Transplant your seedlings from their punnets, taking care not to disturb the root growth. Water in well.

Strawberry plants send out runners, or offshoots, that can be removed and planted elsewhere. The runners will send out new roots at certain points of the growth, so cut them off and transplant them. Cutting off these runners also concentrates the plant's energy on producing fruit.

Feeding and mulching

To improve plant health, feed once a fortnight with liquid seaweed fertiliser. After planting, mulch well with lucerne hay or pea straw to a depth of 5 cm to prevent the fruit from making contact with the soil and rotting.

Watering

In the first month, while the plants are establishing, water 2–3 times a week. Keep well-watered but avoid overwetting the foliage, as this will make it susceptible to fungal diseases. While the plants are producing the strawberries, they will appreciate extra watering.

Harvesting

Hand-pick strawberries when they are a deep, ripe red and before the birds and (potentially) ants get to them. Netting them during the harvesting period will save a lot of ripe strawberries from your bird neighbours. And be wary of kids picking them as you discuss political issues or religion.

Strawberries are perennials that should stay in your patch for up to 3 years. Once fruiting has finished, cut off all runners and any dead leaf matter and apply fresh compost. Overcrowded runners strangle the productivity of strawberry plants, so make this part of your seasonal routine.

SWEDE

First found growing wild in Sweden, the swede is believed to be a naturally occurring hybrid of the turnip and cabbage. The name the Swedish use to describe it, *kålrot*, literally means 'cabbage root'.

Swede is a relatively easy vegetable to grow, occupies little space and stores well in the ground. Considering its origins, it's not surprising that it is cold-hardy and frost-tolerant. It also grows well with little direct sunlight, tolerating heavier soils, so it is suitable for that shady part of your patch where other plants will struggle.

There are varieties that have adapted to cope with warmer conditions, so varietal selection will depend on where you live.

Botanical name
Brassica napobrassica

Family
Brassicaceae (Mustard family)

Origin
Southern and Central Europe

Little Veggie Patch favourite
Champion Purple Top

Space needs
Suited to smaller pots

Companion plant
Silverbeet

How to grow
Sow seed directly into the patch

When to plant
> Zone 1: August–September + January–March
> Zone 2: January–April
> Zone 3: January–May
> Zone 4: March–April

Soil preparation
Likes a moderately fertile soil, although excessive nutrition will cause forking of the roots. If you grow swede in the spot previously used to grow lettuce, the residual nutrition should be adequate. Turn over the soil and fork through compost as part of your preparation.

pH level
6.0–7.0

Position
Shade-tolerant

Spacing
15–20 cm

Problems
Powdery mildew, snails and slugs

SWEDE

Plant seed at a depth of 1–2 cm, then backfill with soil and water in. Once the seedlings germinate, thin out to keep the spacings at approximately 15–20 cm.

Feeding and mulching

Swedes will get by on soil enriched with compost, and won't require additional nutrition during the growing season. Mulch with pea straw or lucerne hay to a depth of 3–5 cm.

Watering

While your seedlings are establishing, they will need watering 2–3 times a week. They are susceptible to lack of moisture, therefore ensure you water them enough to keep the soil from drying out.

Harvesting

Fully mature roots take some months to develop, although you can pick them when you deem the size sufficient — anywhere from a tennis ball upwards. Use a garden fork to loosen the soil and dislodge the swedes.

In cooler areas, swedes store well in the ground, so it is best to leave them in the patch until they are ready to harvest. You can also leave them in the ground and harvest the leafy greens over a long period, but the root will become tough and fibrous, and thus unsuitable for consumption.

SWEETCORN

Sweetcorn is the only member of the maize family that is eaten when the kernels are soft and immature — that is, in their milk stage. All other corns are harvested when the kernels are dry and hard (dent stage), and are primarily used as grain feed.

All corn varieties cross-pollinate among themselves, so more plants will result in better pollination. You will need to plant at least 20 stalks to ensure good cross-pollination and full kernelling of the cobs.

As the name suggests, sweetcorn has a particularly high sugar content, which makes it an ideal vegetable to cook on the barbeque, as slightly charring the cobs enhances their sweetness. This also makes it suitable for the part-time barbequer who has the tendency to lose track of time; however, note that completely charring the cobs will just make them taste burnt.

Botanical name
Zea mays

Family
Poaceae (Maize family)

Origin
South America

Little Veggie Patch favourite
Early Gem

Space needs
Best grown in an in-ground veggie patch

Companion plants
Bean

How to grow
Sow directly into the patch

When to plant
> Zone 1: October–January
> Zone 2: September–February
> Zone 3: August–March
> Zone 4: Any time

Soil preparation
Corn is a greedy feeder, so you will need to prepare a rich soil. Add compost and fresh manure, and allow to settle for a fortnight before planting.

pH level
5.5–7.0

Position
Full sun, with protection from wind. Remember that corn is a large plant that casts a long shadow, so position accordingly.

Spacing
20–30 cm

Problem
Poor pollination

Plant seed directly into the patch once temperatures are sufficiently warm, as cool weather will stunt growth. Use a pencil or chopstick to form holes 5 cm deep and plant 2 seeds in each hole, then backfill with soil and water in. The pollination of sweetcorn is greatly improved when there are at least 20 plants. To improve the rate of pollination, sow even numbers of rows and columns in a block format, rather than in a couple of long rows. Once the seeds have germinated, you will need to thin them out. Be careful not to dislodge the seedlings you intend to keep.

Feeding and mulching

As your plants grow, build up their growing area with compost. This will encourage a stronger root structure that will help the plants support their own weight. The compost will also provide nutrients. Mulch with pea straw or lucerne hay to a depth of 3–5 cm.

Watering

Water your corn 2–3 times a week initially, then give them one good soaking a week thereafter. When the cobs start to form, increase watering to help develop juicy, well-formed kernels.

Harvesting

Corn cobs are ready for harvest about 4 weeks after they flower. The browning off of the silk protruding from the cob indicates it is fully developed and ready for picking. To harvest, twist by hand and pull down.

WATER

'One fine day I was at home, cooking a meal in the early hours of the afternoon, the house intoxicatingly calm and peacefully quiet. The plan was to sink deeper and deeper into a night of care-free laze and then see if I could fool myself into thinking I was on holidays when I woke up the next morning — the true test of your relaxation powers. It was approaching sign-off time, somewhere between 6 and 7 in the evening, and I thought I had beaten society when a pitter-patter of steady, soft knocking and muffled voices came from the front door: 'Zio...Zio!... Zio Mat...Zio!!!!!!'

When I opened the door, it was worse than I had imagined. My nephews Charlie and Sam were not just their energetic, excited selves, they also had water pistols, and they were decent ones. Mum had obviously lashed out, and the quality of the water stream was breathtaking, literally, so who could blame the little guys for wanting to hammer their Zio.

I realised that my night was over, and they were too pumped up for me to play the 'I'm tired' or 'I'm busy' or 'I'm sick' card, so we ventured into the backyard and into the kids' domain. Elise, my sister, had also lashed out on some quality cider, so not all was lost, and we sat down and caught the last of the sun.

As I tried to focus the boys' efforts away from me, encouraging them to give my patch a much needed drink, I noticed a great number of aphids roaming around my patch, particularly on the tomato crop. Elise, now a resourceful mother, formulated a brilliant plan of killing two birds with one stone — the kids would fill their pistols with a mix of soapy water and go about destroying the aphid population. For the next hour the boys exhausted themselves and the aphids with unrelenting slaughter, while Elise and I enjoyed our ciders.

Once the dust had settled, I sank back into my life as a stress-free uncle, believing as only an uncle without kids can — that the difficulties and challenges of parenthood are incredibly overhyped.'

—MP

Water games

Games and water go hand in hand. One thing we have noticed is that kids can be greatly occupied by any activity that wastes water. The genius is in turning that water waste into something useful. Well done, Elise.

For this game you will need:

> water pistols (or water sprays for those who don't like to condone gun use)

> biodegradable detergent, or other organic liquid pest remedy

> water

1

Identify the pest at hand.

2

Word up the soldiers at your disposal and introduce them to their targets. Get them comfortable with the equipment.

3

Create your liquid remedy. Fill the pistols with the mix and take aim.

5

...et them loose!

Kids have attention spans shorter than yours, so you may need to remind them of the target and mission at hand.

Once the mission is completed, thoroughly rinse out the water pistols.

TOMATO

The tomato is the single most important vegetable in Little Veggie Patch Co's life and part of our DNA. Some of our first memories are the smell of towering tomato plants in our Nonnas and Nonnos' vegetable gardens, and these days it is almost impossible to walk past one without rubbing its leaves in our fingers and agitating its scent.

When tomatoes are in season we are obsessed, and when they are not, we are lost. Buying tomatoes when they are out of season continues to be the bane of our existence, as there is no greater disparity in taste than between a home-grown tomato and those you find in the supermarket. Each year, during the harvesting period of March and April, our families go hunting for the perfect pulping tomato ('Roma' works very well), and we make a year's supply of homemade pasta sauce, known as *sugo* (see page 194).

The first varieties of tomato known to humans were yellow; however, we have since favoured the red varieties, which saw them eventually become the standard. So much so that 'red' and 'tomato' have become one of the most popular word associations.

Botanical name
Lycopersicon esculentum

Family
Solanaceae (Nightshade family)

Origin
South America

Little Veggie Patch favourite
Black Russian

Space needs
Suited to larger pots, but prefer an in-ground veggie patch

Companion plants
Basil, marigold

How to grow
Propagate in seed trays

When to plant
> Zone 1: October–December
> Zone 2: August –December
> Zone 3: August–January
> Zone 4: April–July

Soil preparation
Tomatoes are very nitrogen-hungry, so prepare the soil by integrating nitrogen-rich pea or broad bean plants into your soil as a green manure. Alternatively, mix compost and chook manure through your patch a fortnight prior to planting.

pH level
5.5–7.5

Position
Choose a sunny, well-drained spot in your patch, preferably a place you haven't grown tomatoes in the previous season.

Spacing
40–60 cm

Problems
Aphids, leaf curl, powdery mildew

A tomato plant is an ideal starting point for inexperienced and space-conscious gardeners, as it can be grown in a pot or hanging basket or sown directly into your patch. Picking your first, fully ripened tomato, still warm from the summer sun, should prove a defining moment in your vegetable gardening life.

Sow seeds in seed trays at a depth of 0.5–1.0 cm, backfill and water in. Keep them indoors overnight to avoid potential frosts. When transplanting your seedlings, be careful not to damage the delicate root growth. Space out at 30 cm — planting more than necessary will give you some margin for error if some seedlings don't take. Plant out each seedling in a deep hole and cover to just above its first leaves, as it will send out extra roots and form a stronger plant.

Most tomato varieties (except the bush type) require staking and will need support from a young age. Make sure that, as the plant grows, it is supported by the trellis structure and doesn't fall over under its own weight, attracting pests and diseases.

Once the plants begin to mature, you will have to cull some seedlings to get spacings at approximately 60 cm.

Your plants will send out flowers early. Pinch these out to transfer energy to the growth of the plant. You should also pinch out the sucker shoots that sprout between the main stem and arm branches. Pinching will help establish a better formed plant with good airflow for fruiting.

Consider setting up some form of shelter from wind, and on hot days, from the sun.

Feeding and mulching

As your tomato plants grow, you will need to supplement their nitrogen needs with an application of liquid seaweed fertiliser once a month. When your plants are about 3 months old, give them an application of potash to help promote good fruit growth.

A fortnight after transplanting, mulch with pea straw or lucerne hay to a depth of 3–5 cm.

Watering

Young seedlings will need watering daily for the first week and then 2–3 times a week for the next fortnight. Overwatering can become a problem with mature plants, so deeper soakings once a week will help encourage stronger root growth and a healthier, happier plant.

Harvesting

The fruit will be ready to harvest when it starts to soften and form its mature colour, dependent on the variety. Picking off the tomatoes by hand should not damage the plant. If you are picking off a cluster of tomatoes you will need secateurs to cut the stem of the cluster.

Nonna's Kitchen

Sugo

> Pick or source well-ripened tomatoes. If they are a little hard, leave them out in the sun for a couple of days. One kilo of tomatoes will make about half a litre of sauce, therefore the quantity depends on your ambition. Mat's household sources about 100 kg each year.

> Boil the tomatoes in a large pot, in batches of around 10 kg, until tender.

> Pass the tomatoes through a pulping machine – this will remove the skin and seeds, leaving you with the tomato pulp.

> Pour the sugo into sterilised jars (or VB bottles), adding a couple of basil leaves before sealing. Once all jars are sealed, boil them for 15–20 minutes in a large pot – this will prevent the sugo from any fermentation, which could cause the sealed jars to explode when stored.

TURNIP

The turnip is a vegetable with an identity crisis, as it borrows characteristics from both the radish and the potato. When raw it has a sharp bite, akin to a radish. When cooked, however, this flavour subsides and begins to resemble that of a potato. It is also commonly confused with the swede.

Turnip greens are used raw in salads but the root is best roasted, as an accompaniment to meats, particularly lamb.

We did say that parsnip was our favourite roasting vegetable, but in truth it could actually be turnip. Hmm, not sure now...

Botanical name
Brassica rapa

Family
Brassicaceae (Mustard family)

Origin
Central and Southern Europe

Little Veggie Patch favourite
Purple Top Milan

Space needs
Suited to smaller pots

Companion plants
Tomato, onion, pea

How to grow
Sow seeds directly into the patch

When to plant
> Zone 1: September–November
       + January–April
> Zone 2: September–April
> Zone 3: August–May
> Zone 4: March–September

Soil preparation
Prefers a well-dug, friable soil that is moderately fertile. Must be free-draining. A week prior to planting, dig through compost and well-rotted manure as part of the soil preparation.

pH level
6.0–7.0

Position
Full sun, but will tolerate some shade. Don't grow where you have grown brassicas in the previous growing season.

Spacing
15–20 cm

Problems
Snails and slugs

TURNIP

Sow seed into the patch at a depth of 0.5–1.0 cm, then backfill with soil and water in. You will need to thin out the seedlings a fortnight after germination. It is best to dispose of the thinned out seedlings in your compost.

Feeding and mulching

Keep the level of organic matter in the soil high to adequately feed the roots, and mulch with pea straw or lucerne hay to a depth of 3–5 cm. Turnips benefit from an application of liquid potash every 2–3 weeks.

Watering

Young seedlings have the tendency to dry out, so regular watering, 2–3 times a week, is important; however, turnip plants will not tolerate poorly drained soil, so ensure that it drains well. Cut back on watering once the plants have established themselves.

Harvesting

Turnips can be harvested when young, at about the size of a radish, or mature, when they will grow as large as a beetroot. Older roots tend to become woody, so it is best to pick them young; stagger your harvest to suit. Turnips store well in the ground except when there is prolific rainfall.

To harvest, dislodge each root with a garden fork and pull out by hand.

Start picking the leaves once the plant is large enough to sustain regular leaf growth, usually after 4–6 weeks.

ZUCCHINI

On a recent road trip from Perth to Melbourne, we needed to find ways of passing the time. Driving games, usually involving cruise control, passed the most time, but among them was a reoccurring A to Z game recalling the types (not varieties!) of the vegetables and edible herbs we knew. No matter how many times we repeated them, we couldn't comprehend that there were no matches for 'I' or 'J' (unlike 'X', which was accepted), and that 'Z', a letter that proved so troublesome in all other forms of the game (bands, car makes, alcoholic drinks), was an absolute given. We felt incredibly privileged to be residing in Australia and not the United Kingdom or New Zealand, where the zucchini is more commonly referred to as the courgette.

The zucchini comes from the same family as squash, and is sometimes referred to as a summer squash. If left to its own devices, the fruit will grow up to a metre in length, but the taste is better and the skin less tough if it is picked earlier. The plant itself grows large (normally 1–1.5 m), with rough and prickly leaves. While a zucchini is an investment in space, particularly for the domestic veggie patch, it can provide a prolific harvest.

On cold autumn nights that signal winter's intent, there is no better activity than preparing the ultimate comfort food, *ratatouille*. Hand-picked zucchini from your veggie garden is therefore an essential.

Botanical name
Cucurbita pepo var. *melopepo*

Family
Cucurbitaceae (Gourd family)

Origin
Central and South America

Little Veggie Patch favourite
Zephyr

Space needs
Best grown in an in-ground veggie patch

Companion plants
Corn, radish, celery

How to grow
Sow directly into the patch

When to plant
> Zone 1: October–December
> Zone 2: September–January
> Zone 3: August–March
> Zone 4: February–September

Soil preparation
A week prior to planting, prepare the soil with lots of compost and organic manure, ensuring that it is fertile and free-draining.

pH level
5.5–6.5

Position
Warm spot in full sun with room to move

Spacing
1 m

ZUCCHINI

Make sure the temperatures are sufficiently warm and that cold days and nights are behind you, as zucchini plants do not appreciate the cold weather. Prepare a small mound of pure compost, then sow the seed directly into the compost at a depth that is 2–3 times its diameter, and water in thoroughly.

When the plant matures, it will be very large and susceptible to gusts of wind that can uproot it and/or damage leaf growth. To protect it against this type of damage, peg down the main stem. Depending on the size of your plant, you may need more than one peg.

Feeding and mulching

Zucchini will benefit from supplementary watering with liquid seaweed fertiliser every fortnight; the compost should also provide plenty of nutrition. Mulch with pea straw or lucerne hay to a depth of 3–5 cm.

Watering

Keep the seedlings well-watered, as the compost should provide perfect drainage. While the plants are establishing over the first month, water 2–3 times a week, then cut back to a longer weekly soaking.

Harvesting

Zucchinis flower and fruit relatively quickly, and can be picked while the flower is still attached to the fruit itself. Cut the fruit from the plant at the stem.

Don't leave the fruit to mature on the vine for too long, as it will become aerated, with tough skin, eventually turning into a tasteless marrow. Picking will also encourage development of new growth.

Nonna's Kitchen

Zucchini flower broken eggs

2 dozen zucchini flowers
olive oil
2 garlic cloves, finely sliced
3 eggs
flat-leaf parsley, coarsely chopped, to serve
good-quality crusty loaf, sliced and toasted
salt and freshly ground black pepper

> Once the zucchini plant's flowers have been allowed to pollinate (a day or two after they have fully opened), pick 2 dozen flowers.

> Wash the flowers thoroughly as there may still be insects doing their 'thang' inside them.

> Heat a frying pan over high heat, add a splash of oil and, when hot, fry the flowers for 1–2 minutes.

> Reduce the heat and add the garlic, season and fry for a further minute or two, being careful to not burn the garlic.

> Crack the eggs into the pan and gently but continuously turn over until cooked (the gentler the better).

> Turn heat off and sprinkle with parsley. Season to taste and serve on toasted crusty loaf.

Serves 2

Snail damage

Possum damage

(Spot the strawberry!)

Rodent damage

Caterpillar damage

Powdery mildew

Nutrient deficiency

Aphids

Fruit fly damage

Aphid damage

PESTS
AND DISEASES

Caterpillars

Gall wasp damage

Slug damage

A common reaction when encountering a pest or disease in your vegetable garden is to bolt out the door, buy a multipurpose, chemically based spray and then hammer the garden. Days later, with the pest nowhere to be seen, you find yourself thanking the forward thinking people of science who manufactured the spray. Maybe you feel like inspecting the carnage too, so you take out your microscope and wander through the garden. Of course, you can see the effectiveness of the spray in the thousands of dead bugs lying face up in your veggie patch, further justifying its merits. However, on closer inspection, among the dead pests are hundreds of good bugs and pest predators that you didn't realise existed — your mind was so preoccupied with the pest at hand you failed to see your garden operating as a bug community, and now good and bad lie slaughtered, side by side. So what are the consequences now?

A war analogy will prove useful at this point, because applying a chemical spray to your garden is very much like making the decision to carpet bomb a city during war. While the bombs are able to wipe out the enemy, the loss of innocent civilian life is unavoidable, as the bombs, no matter how precise they are, cannot differentiate between good and bad at ground level. The city is also left devastated, and those civilians who survive the bombing will need to rebuild their

lives, sometimes with horrific injuries, among the ruins — a lengthy and trying process.

Now bombs have come a long way since their origins, but the main development in bomb technology has been the improvement in their ability to kill, still indiscriminately. There is no bomb that is able to target bad and avoid good — collateral damage is always a by-product. The same applies to chemical sprays.

When chemical sprays were first developed there was a tendency to go to war at the slightest sign of unrest — sometimes compounding the problem or exacerbating another, which would then provide justification for using more sprays. Any attempt by the organic gardener to mediate and address the issue holistically was perceived as ignorance of the issue at hand, or weak or unpatriotic, and this went on for a number of years, until the 1950s and '60s, when those using sprays finally recognised the untold damage they were causing.

Since then food-growers have been trying to find a balance in their practices. The advent of IPM — integrated pest management — accepts that there must be a more holistic approach to pest management, including better identification and targeting of pests, better timing of applications, using natural defences and introducing biological controls (predators) and 'softer' chemicals. While IPM is a large improvement on old practices, it has only come half way and there is still a feeling that spraying, to some degree, is a necessity.

ORGANIC APPROACH

Organic gardening does not condone war, nor is it unrealistic in believing a perfect world can exist. Instead it strives towards creating a realistic world, one that is in general harmony, accepting that there will be good and there will be bad, but if an ideal environment is created, the balance will be greatly in good's favour. For example, take the country we live in, Australia. Sure there are some unpleasant people in the ranks and a few truly appalling human beings, but generally people are open-minded and pleasant and civil, and we have systems that control and deal with the bad facets so this country is a good place in which to live. The garden world is no different.

Pest and disease control in your vegetable garden requires a proactive, attentive and holistic approach to the environment in which your plants and all pests and predators live. Following some basic Gardening 101 guidelines will ensure your plants' natural defensive mechanics are in fine working order and that a society of predators, and pests, can operate and help your plants thrive.

Paying careful attention to your garden

Being up close and personal with your garden and those operating within it will help you understand who is doing what job. Grabbing a microscope and inspecting your veggie patch will make you privy to the abundance of insect life going about their daily business. Among them are pests and predators, good and bad. Sometimes a pest, while appearing nasty and troublesome, may actually be a predator in disguise! It's not black and white.

Good garden hygiene

Any over-ripening or rotten fruit and decaying plant matter will be food for a variety of pests, so it is important to keep your garden free of these materials. Weeds can be a breeding ground for some pests, so regularly remove them and maintain a thick layer of mulch to help suppress them.

Regular watering practices

Inconsistent and erratic watering practices promote disease in plants as well as poor fruit development. Use an automated drip irrigation system to ensure your plants are receiving regular drinks that penetrate directly to the roots. Avoid using fan sprays that leave the foliage wet, as this can lead to infection. If the weather has been especially wet or dry, amend your watering to suit.

In small gardens, where irrigation systems become too costly to justify, watering in the morning is not only best but will also give you a chance to interact with the garden.

Pests and diseases tend to strike when your plants are most susceptible — when they are either thirsty or horribly drunk. By satisfying your plants' drinking needs you will greatly reduce the incidence of problems in the patch.

Mulch

Applying organic mulches, such as lucerne hay and pea straw, will suppress weeds, lock in moisture, feed your plants and make life difficult for pest activity. A no-brainer.

Good soil health

A soil that is fertile and drains properly reduces the chance of attack by pests and diseases. Fertilise regularly, but not excessively, and ensure that your plants' nutrient requirements are sufficiently met.

Crop rotation practices

Some pests and diseases will target one species of plant, so subsequent infections will be greatly reduced by practising crop rotation, which is also a method of amending and improving the distribution of essential nutrients within the soil.

When you're rotating crops in the veggie patch, don't just change the individual type of vegetable, but all plants that belong to that family of vegetables — for example, the family Brassicaceae, which includes cauliflower, cabbage, broccoli and kale, or the Solanaceae family of tomatoes, eggplants, chillies and potatoes. This is because pests and diseases are often associated with all plants within a genus.

The use of green manures is also recommended. It refers to the practice of growing plants to return nutrients back into the soil. Green manures are primarily legumes (for example, peas), which feed the soil with nitrogen, while other veggies, such as tomatoes, draw it out.

Good airflow

Avoid overcrowding your plants, or planting in damp, humid areas that are the perfect breeding grounds for disease. Space your crops properly and make sure you thin them out where necessary.

Diversify your plant species

A diverse range of fruit trees, vegetables, herbs and flowers will attract a diverse range of insects. Some will be predators that will naturally control other pests and help keep your veggie patch in balance. In small vegetable gardens, plant diversity should be a given.

Special care during susceptible periods

Meet plants' nutrient and watering requirements during critical periods of growth, particularly during fruiting, when they will demand more of both. After periods of extreme heat or rainfall, you will have to adapt and recognise the changing needs of your plants.

Use organic methods of control

There are always organic methods of preventing and controlling pests and diseases, and these should be your first port of call. Avoid using chemically based sprays that focus on providing short-term solutions to the detriment of the long-term health of your veggie patch.

PESTS

Ants

Ants work in highly organised colonies that can be up to a million soldiers strong. The characteristic 'ant trail' is formed because ants leave behind a scent that allows the rest of the colony to follow.

There are thousands of ant species in Australia, but the most common one in the house and garden is the black house ant. While they can appear unsightly, ants can largely be considered a beneficial insect. They help clean food and garden waste and kill garden pests; one of the first examples of an introduced predator, they were used to help control pests in ancient China.

The first step in dealing with ants as pests is to identify the trouble they are creating. Ants perform two undesirable functions in the garden:

1 They consume the honeydew left behind by aphids and whiteflies, valuing this source of food so greatly that they protect these pests; and

2 they attack and infest some sweet ripening fruits.

Ant attack is easily recognised by the infestation of hundreds or thousands of ants on your crops, so you won't have any trouble identifying the problem.

Watch out for your newly sown seeds — ants love to steal them. If you notice ants around, their friends, the aphids, usually won't be far away.

Organic solution

If ants are causing problems in your garden, try disrupting their scent trail by using eucalyptus oil, garlic, lemon juice, tea-tree oil or any other strongly scented substance. Create scent barriers around your crops that will confuse the ants' line of attack.

If an ant colony is proving too resistant, try pouring boiling water mixed with your household detergent in the nest.

Good garden hygiene will deprive ants of a food source and generally control populations setting up their battlefields near your garden.

Aphids

The aphid is as close a companion to the tomato plant as basil; however, unlike basil, the aphid is the menacing, annoying companion you wish didn't exist.

Aphids are small black or green bugs, usually with wings, about 1 mm long. They feed on the tender young growth of plants that generally have a high water content, such as tomato and squash, sucking out the life of the plant from the inside out. When feeding, they secrete a sap, known as honeydew, which is then fed on by a yeast-like fungus called sooty mould, making the leaves look as if they are covered in black soot. Honeydew is also a favourite of ants, which protect the aphids — their source of honeydew. Aphids reproduce extremely quickly and, almost before your eyes, can infest your crops.

Organic solution

To help avert an aphid problem, make sure your plants are well-watered and not over-fertilised with nitrogen. The best natural predator of the aphid is the ladybird, so try attracting a high ladybird population by planting mustard greens, dill, fennel and coriander.

Nasturtiums are a great companion plant to help control the aphid population and distract them from your prized crops. Every gardener should incorporate nasturtiums as a natural defence against a number of common veggie garden pests, including snails and slugs. Garlic also works well as a companion plant, as do marigolds.

Use sticky yellow traps to help indicate when you have an aphid problem. Spray the affected plants with a soapy mix of water, made by using generic household dishwashing detergent diluted in water at a ratio of 1:10.

Birds

If you do a stocktake of the birds roaming your garden, 90% are bound to be friendly. They are the pest controllers and pollinators that contribute to the balance of your mini-ecosystem. The other 10% aren't so friendly — they quite often rip and dislodge seedlings, dig great holes in your patch and attack your ripe fruit. These birds can be a real pain.

Bird damage is easy to identify, and you will quite often catch them in the act. Last season we came across a pair of European blackbirds eating the ripening 'Black Russian' tomatoes in our patch and we lost it. We spent the next three hours constructing an impenetrable bird net.

Other signs of bird damage are large gaping holes in your soil and the mysterious disappearance of entire seedlings. In reality the bird was probably trying to pick off a leaf and underestimated its own strength.

Organic solution

Before undertaking any course of action, it is important to know your bird enemies:

> common myna

> European blackbird

> common starling

Like all creatures, birds have their enemies too. When your area is devoid of predatory birds, you may consider a fake version. Ever wondered why people place fake owls or cats in their patches? This may work, or at least initially, until the troublemakers realise the owl is in fact a plastic toy.

Bird control is your one great opportunity to make a killer scarecrow (see page 149), which will hopefully be more effective than banging on the window when you spot a troublemaker. Get as creative as possible — the more the scarecrow is able to react with the breeze, emitting noises and sharp light, the more effective a deterrent it will be. Hang CDs and chimes from your scarecrow. (Our scarecrow is really a fashion scarecrow, not a work scarecrow...)

Pets will also be effective deterrents. The more active the pet, the more likely they are to distract the birds and save your crops from meaningful damage.

Netting, fine enough so it cannot be penetrated by the smallest birds, is a comprehensive safeguard for your vegetables and fruit trees. While it is relatively inexpensive over small gardens, it can be costly to set up over larger ones, so explore your other options first. To avoid injuring birds or bats, make sure the netting is taut when you set it up.

Caterpillars

Caterpillars are the larvae of a wide range of butterfly and moth species. While it is a beautiful sight to see butterflies enjoying the colours and fragrances of your veggie patch. The most common visitor is the menacing white cabbage moth, and its close relative, the white cabbage butterfly, both real pests as their caterpillars can be a real nuisance in the garden.

Identifying these pests is easy, as they are a vivid white and particularly attracted to your brassica crops, such as cabbage (from which they derive their names), broccoli, cauliflower and brussel sprouts. It is not the moth that does the damage, but the larvae, which are smooth green caterpillars. These critters house themselves in the protective growth of your cabbage leaves or broccoli heads and feast from the inside out, leaving gaping holes in your crops.

The tomato grub is a type of caterpillar that does its best work harvesting in your ripening fruit.

Organic solution

To prevent the caterpillars from munching their way through your crops, you will need to prevent the moths from laying their eggs in the first place. The most effective method is to construct a physical barrier, such as fine netting, especially over younger crops, when a small meal can be critical to the life and death of a plant. If you come across the problem too late and find the caterpillars infesting your crops, you will need to engage the kids in an activity of search and destroy. A hand-picking ground war against these caterpillars is your best avenue of action.

Try planting white flowers or make some fake decoy butterflies out of plastic. White cabbage moths are believed to have poor eyesight and will not enter a territory already occupied by another.

In the worst cases, you can use *Bacillus thuringiensis* (BT), which is a biological alternative to a pesticide. This measure, considered safe, is used in organic farming.

Healthy plants can often outgrow the damage done by these caterpillars, so ensure you are properly servicing the nutrient and water demands of your crops.

Earwigs

Although the earwig bears no resemblance to an ear dressed in a bad toupée, it is not a great looking insect. There is a traditional belief that it takes pleasure in entering the ear canal and burrowing its way into the brain, hence its name. There are more than 60 types of earwigs native to Australia, most of them harmless to your vegetable garden. It is the introduced European species that can be a problem child. Saying that, the damage that earwigs do to your crops is not at the same level as some other, more devastating, pests.

Earwigs prefer wet, cooler conditions to the dry heat of summer, so this is when they are most prevalent. Mostly nocturnal, they can be found hiding in dark and moist areas during the daytime — typically under pots or bricks piled up in the corner. They feed on other insects and mostly dead or decomposing plant matter; however, they will sometimes go for your tender, younger seedlings.

Organic solution

When considering earwig control, you need to first ascertain whether your earwig population is doing more bad than good, as they can also help control aphids and other pests.

Like caterpillars, earwigs leave irregular holes or eat the edges of leaf growth. They are also known to eat through the stems of new growth. To distinguish caterpillar damage from earwig damage, look for the webbing or excrement that indicates a caterpillar's presence.

Practising good garden hygiene is one preventive method of ensuring that dead matter is composted instead of being left lying around the veggie patch. If you have decided that earwigs are responsible for the damage

to your veggies and you want to eliminate them, lure them by filling up a bucket with water and then applying 20–30 mm of raw linseed oil to create a film of oil on top. This should attract and then kill many earwigs.

You can also try placing scrunched up newspaper in an old bowl, which you should leave overnight in the garden, turned upside down. The next day, empty the contents in boiling water.

Fruit flies

There are three common types of fruit fly in Australia — the Queensland fruit fly, which is native to the east coast; the Mediterranean fruit fly, a species confined to Western Australia; and the cucumber fruit fly. The cucumber fruit fly's diet revolves around pumpkin, melons and zucchini, all members of the cucurbit family, while the Mediterranean and Queensland fruit flies feed on a wider variety of crops, including figs, cherries and other stone fruits, apples, pears, guavas, feijoas, tomatoes and capsicums.

The female fruit fly lays its eggs within the skin of the fruit, and the hatching larvae, white maggot-looking creatures, eat the inside of the fruit, causing them to rot and fall from the tree. Once the larvae are fully grown, they leave the rotten fruit to burrow into the soil and pupate — spinning a cocoon and eventually turning into a fruit fly. The process then continues itself. Fruit flies are a bigger pest in warmer regions than cooler climates, as they generally prefer to breed in warm temperatures.

Organic solution

Identifying and disposing of infected fruit is important in breaking the cycle. If the fruit develops dimples in it, or is weeping a clear sap, then the larvae have already hatched, so pick the affected fruit and destroy it. Fruit prematurely rotting on the tree or vine is another telltale sign.

Garden hygiene is the key to preventing a fruit fly problem. Make sure that vegetables and fruit are not left to over-ripen and then rot on the tree or vine. Avoid planting vegetables and fruit you don't plan to eat. Keep your fruit trees well pruned, and consider planting dwarf rootstock or espaliering fruit trees to make them easier to harvest.

In terms of controlling the pest, you can hang traps from fruit trees and around the garden to capture and kill the fruit flies, but these will only kill relatively small numbers. Another type of trap uses red wine vinegar, which is poured into a shallow plate and covered with plastic wrap. You then poke small holes in the plastic so that the fruit flies will fly into it but be unable to escape.

An effective but time-consuming measure is to cover individual fruit or whole trees in exclusion bags, which the fruit fly cannot penetrate.

In the southern states, excluding Western Australia, the fruit fly will not be as great a concern as up north, where you may even need to consider avoiding planting susceptible plants.

Gall wasps

The gall wasp is a tiny species of wasp, approximately 1–8 mm long, which lays its eggs on the inside of the semi-mature branches of lemon or grapefruit trees. After the eggs are laid, their housing develops into a swelling or gall that can be easily seen. A completely closed gall means the eggs have yet to hatch, while a gall with tiny dots signifies the wasps have hatched and left.

Organic solution

Controlling gall wasp takes a combined community effort. The prolific, migratory nature of the gall wasp means that if your neighbour's tree is infected, then inevitably yours will also succumb. The only way to eradicate the gall wasp is to cut out all the affected branches and properly dispose of them; however, if your neighbour doesn't do the same, all that effort will be in vain.

Gall wasp will not kill your citrus tree but it will diminish its productivity and appearance, making it look spindly and bare. Yellow sticky traps on and around your citrus will reduce their numbers, but once your tree is infected, your only option is to cut back the affected branches and dispose of them.

Gall wasps require constant management, which includes hard pruning every few years. Prune in late winter or early spring, before the gall wasps hatch. Cut right back to the most recent swelling.

Leaf miners

Leaf miner is the name given to the larvae of an insect, usually flies but sometimes moths and beetles, that live in and eat the leaf tissue of a plant. These insects lay their eggs just below the epidermis of the leaf, where they ultimately hatch as larvae and feed. Eggs may appear as raised small spots on the leaves.

Once in the tissue, the leaf miners are largely protected from predators and sprays, so the issue here is controlling the pests that lay such larvae in the first place. The damage of a leaf miner is easily recognised — lines or mine tracks trailed by the black faecal material or frass it leaves behind. If you notice leaf miner damage, pick off and dispose of the infected leaves.

Organic solution

Healthy plants can generally withstand and outgrow the attack of a leaf miner, so ensuring you are properly caring for your plants' nutrient and water requirements is an important strategy in dealing with this pest. Also try putting out yellow sticky traps to catch the adult flies that are responsible for laying the eggs. Mulching the ground below your plants will help impede the larvae's progress through your soil, where they pupate and hatch as mature insects. This will stop the vicious cycle.

As a control method, make your own pest oil by mixing 1 cup of vegetable oil with 1 teaspoon of dishwashing liquid. Then dilute at 40:1 with water and spray on the affected foliage.

Encouraging predators such as ladybirds and parasitic wasps will also help control leaf miner.

Possums

Possums take out two prestigious pest awards — the Cutest and Most Damaging. These smiling assassins of the vegetable garden can destroy an entire newly planted veggie patch in a couple of effortless big nights out.

As possums are territorial, they most likely resided in your area before your vegetable patch or fruit orchard, so don't feel as if they have set up a life intent on mocking and hassling you. If you have the deviant (and illegal) idea of murdering your possum neighbours or relocating them to another neighbourhood, be aware that another family will kindly take up the vacancy, and business will resume as usual. Therefore you need to look at managing your life alongside theirs rather than concoct ways to eradicate them.

It is not difficult to ascertain when a possum has struck. If you notice possums playing in the trees around your patch one night and then completely devoured veggie seedlings the next, put two and two together and it does make four.

Organic solution

Possums are nocturnal, so active at night. One defence is your pet dog, who we guarantee is a possumacist and will bark from dusk to dawn if given the chance, but we're certain both you and your neighbour will place greater value on a good night's sleep, so this is not a long-term solution.

There are lots of other ideas for deterring or distracting possums:

> sensor lights
> high-frequency transmitters (they may also freak out your dog)
> leaving out alternative meals
> a commercial possum repellent
> chilli sprays
> garlic sprays
> eucalyptus spray

The number of remedies that are continually developed for the market indicates that possums are adaptable creatures, which evolve faster than we give them credit for. Before last year's Melbourne International Flower and Garden Show, we were advocates of chilli/garlic spray until we noticed the possums had devoured all the jalapeño chillies in our display in one night!

For a stinky deterrent, stuff some blood and bone into an old stocking to form a ball, then place it along the path the possums like to take to your veggie patch. No one likes hanging around a veggie patch that stinks, not even possums.

The only foolproof fix for managing possums is to build a physical barrier they can't penetrate. Bird netting properly secured around your patch will do the job. Possum damage is most detrimental when your seedlings are young, and there will come a time when your plants are large enough to withstand and not suffer as a result of a feed: plants that are 4–6 weeks old should be mature enough to withstand possum feedings.

You can also place plastic guards around the lower trunks of adolescent fruit trees that might be prone to being ring-barked by possums.

Rodents

Active night hunters, mice and rats can wreak just as much damage as possums, and are sometimes harder to control.

The damage left behind by rodents is similar to that of the possum — whole seedlings can be reduced to rubble or adolescent fruit trees decimated. A client recently went to the enormous effort of safeguarding their vegetable garden from possums only to find that large rats were responsible for most of the trouble, including the ring-barking of their fruit trees.

To identify rodent damage, look for their droppings, which will differentiate them from other pests. Rodents have smaller, pellet-like droppings (about 1 cm across for rats, mice about half that), while possum droppings are less consistent in size and shape, but generally bigger. If you have noticed rats or mice in the house, they are just as likely to be roaming around the garden. Rodents have the ability to penetrate physical barriers by chewing through them, so investigate netting for such damage. They can also burrow under netting and other barriers, so the defence against rodents is a holistic approach in regard to garden hygiene.

Organic solution

Fruit rotting on the ground or on the plants is an open invitation to these unwanted guests, so maintain a meticulous garden. Manage your compost properly and don't load your compost pile with scraps that can't be composted.

Avoid using poisonous traps in the garden, as they can contaminate your patch. Pet cats and dogs are natural predators, so *rodent patrol* is a definite 'pro' when you are considering integrating a pet into your family.

The best way to naturally contain rodents is to build a diverse and healthy garden that attracts predators, such as birds and non-poisonous snakes, to control their numbers.

Spring-loaded mouse and rat traps, remember those?

Root-knot nematodes

Also known as eelworm, root-knot nematode is a common garden pest that operates within your soil. While the actual pest is so small and translucent that it is almost impossible to see, evidence of their work can be identified by the small galls on the plant's roots, where the larvae feed and drain nutrients while restricting the plant's ability to use water and fertiliser effectively. Root-knot nematode will result in poor plant growth, reduction in the quality and yield of the fruit, and increased susceptibility to other diseases and stresses.

Organic solution

Plants that are particularly susceptible to root-knot nematodes include tomato, potato, carrot, parsnip, silverbeet and lettuce. To reduce the likelihood of this pest striking, practise good crop rotation, and don't leave mature plants in the soil for too long. Weeds can host root-knot nematodes, so keep your veggie beds weed-free.

Marigolds are a good companion plant that will help control and reduce their numbers. They should be reintegrated into the soil as a green manure at the end of their season.

Keep the level of organic matter in your soil high to ensure your plants receive sufficient nutrition, which means they will be less susceptible to infestation.

As the symptoms of this pest are contained within the soil, you will probably not come across it until you are removing crops — which may then explain poor growth or yield. If you discover diseased plants, do not compost them, but dispose of them in a plastic bag, then place the bag in your general waste bin. Dig out all the root matter of the crop to ensure you have removed most of the nematodes and their food.

Scale

Scale is the name given to a type of pest that sucks on the sap of plant leaves, excreting honeydew, which ants consume. It is another pest that is protected by the ant because of this valuable substance.

There are a number of different types of scale, including black scale, soft brown scale, red scale and cottony cushion scale; each name reflects its appearance on the plant.

Scale damage can be seen in malnutrition in your plants' leaves, which usually turn yellow first, then drop from the plant. Sooty mould is another by-product of the damage. The pest itself is an oval, legless critter, approximately 2–5 mm in diameter, which attaches itself to the leaf with tiny suction cups that it uses to feed. They are mostly found on the undersides or at the joints of leaves.

Organic solution

Controlling ant populations will help you control scale, making them more susceptible to the natural predators that will feed on them. Excessive nitrogen in your soil, on the other hand, will promote scale feeding, as there will be more new foliage, so be sure to monitor your fertilisation practices.

A preventive method of scale control is to spray a solution of water and baking soda, mixed in a ratio of 10:1, over your susceptible plants in winter. Fruit trees, particularly citrus, are targets of scale infestation.

You can easily remove scale by scraping them off with a rag dipped in a soapy solution of 10 parts water to 1 part soap. Adding alcohol, such as methylated spirits, to the solution will make it more effective, but be careful, as some delicate plants may not react well. Add alcohol to the mix at 1:3.

Ladybirds and parasitic wasps are the main predators of scale.

Snails and slugs

Snails and slugs are molluscs that have left the aquatic environment and evolved to survive on the land, but they still require damp, sheltered areas in order to survive. They produce slime to enable them to move along the ground and to protect their bodies from drying out. In an old share house, we would often notice slime trails on our living room rug after especially dry periods — the snails would have been seeking moisture and protection. Occasionally, after a night out, one of us would return home to encounter, first hand, the slugs doing their business on our cherished rug, so we'd fetch the saltshaker and excitedly wake the other flatmates. In the share house snails and slugs provide mystique and a meaningful house-bonding activity, but in the veggie patch they are major pests.

Organic solution

Slugs and snails can consume your veggies at different stages of their growth, but they prefer the softer fruits and the younger, sweeter growth of seedlings. They are active night hunters when the conditions are more favourable, and they tend to be gregarious, returning to the same resting place. For this reason you can concentrate your eradication efforts on the same haunts and usually be successful. The favourite resting places of snails and slugs tend to be under stones, logs and any protective canopy that locks in moisture. As snails have protective shells, they will generally remain above ground, so they are more easily spotted than slugs, which can burrow under the soil for protection.

The home veggie garden is an ideal feeding ground for these pests, as it is well-watered and offers an array of tender plant and fruit growth for them to feed on. There are a number of methods you can use to help control these pests.

> Good garden hygiene is important in removing potential resting spots.

> They find it difficult to move over rougher ground, so try sprinkling sawdust over the soil to restrict their movement.

> Hand-picking at night, when they are on the move, is effective. You can lure them out with an afternoon watering session or go hunting after rain. Dispose of the bodies properly, as their eggs can still hatch. It's best to leave them in the sun to dry out or throw them over your nosey neighbour's fence.

> Use ideal resting spots as traps, such as a wooden board on top of two bricks. Or grow nasturtiums to provide a great damp canopy. Go about picking off and disposing.

> Make beer traps by half burying glasses of beer in the ground — the smell of fermenting beer will attract them and they will drown in the liquid.

> Physical barriers, such as fine mesh cages, will keep them away from your prized seedlings.

> Stinging nettle and basil work as companion plants in repelling snails and slugs.

> Make a spray of 50% vinegar and 50% water, increasing the concentration of vinegar if the spray is not successful. It is best to spray the soil around the susceptible plants rather than the leaves of the plant themselves.

> What to do with the left over coffee? Dilute it in water (1:10) and spray on the foliage of young seedlings. This will help ward off snails, as caffeine is toxic to them. You can also sprinkle used coffee granules around the plants.

Thrips

Thrips are tiny, slender insects, no more than 1 mm long, which feed on plants by puncturing the leaves and then sucking out the water and nutrients, leaving speckled discolouration or complete browning when there is a heavy infestation. Look out for the damage of thrips on crops such as beans, onion and squash.

Due to the size of thrips, first identify the telltale damage before venturing into the veggie patch with a magnifying glass to confirm your suspicions — it is generally restricted to leaf growth. Its behaviour is not dissimilar to that of leaf miners.

Organic solution

Thrips are attracted to bright pink and blue, so sticky traps in these colours can be useful for catching the adults.

Encourage strong plant growth so that your crops will outgrow any damage caused by the thrips. Also encourage their predators, such as ladybirds, into the garden.

Thrips are more prevalent in the greenhouse than in the veggie patch, so practise good garden hygiene in and around your greenhouse to control their numbers. Keep the greenhouse weed-free, as it is a favourite hiding place. Air it out during the heat of summer every couple of years. Exposing it to high temperatures will eliminate any thrip problems you may have.

You can actually buy good bugs over the internet to release into your garden. Here are a couple of sites worth looking at:

> http://www.ecoorganicgarden.com.au/gg.php
> http://www.ipmtechnologies.com.au

Whiteflies

The whitefly is a common pest all over Australia and one that we are learning to live with. There are three different types of whitefly active in our country — the greenhouse, cabbage and silverleaf. As the names of the greenhouse and the cabbage whitefly suggest, they are more active in greenhouses and on brassica crops, respectively. The silverleaf whitefly is known to attack up to 250 species of plants.

The whitefly is a small, white flying insect about 1–2 mm long. If you disturb a plant and see hundreds of small white flies jump and swirl before calmly resettling on your crops as though nothing has happened, you have whitefly. They lay their eggs on the underside of leaves and change colour from yellowy white to brown within a few days. Cabbage and greenhouse whiteflies lay their eggs in arches and circles, while silverleaf whiteflies lay theirs in a more random arrangement.

All whiteflies damage crops in the same fashion (similar to that of aphids), as their larvae feed and suck sap from the leaf growth and then secrete a sticky substance, known as honeydew, which restricts the normal growth of the plant and causes leaves to turn yellow and mottle. Honeydew can then become infested by black sooty mould, which can in turn affect the plants' ability to photosynthesise. Whiteflies can also inadvertently transmit disease to your plants. The life cycle of this pest accelerates in summer, when it can become a serious problem.

Organic solution

The best way to prevent whitefly is to avoid leaving mature crops in the ground. Install sticky yellow traps near your crops to alert you of a whitefly population, then once you have identified them (shake a plant or two to check), spray a soapy mix over the affected plants (see page 212). Early detection will help you to keep these pests under control. Manually removing and disposing of the infected leaves as soon as you notice them is another option.

At the end of a growing season when whitefly has been a problem, let your growing space stand idle for a week or more to starve the remaining population.

White cabbage moth (see Caterpillars)

DISEASES

Blossom end rot

This disease attacks fruit as it sets on the plant, forming a sunken and discoloured spot on the fruit's end, which eventually leads to premature rotting. It is a cruel form of punishment for the part-time gardener, as blossom end rot can result from a number of factors:

> inconsistent watering;
> extreme weather conditions (too dry or too wet);
> excessive nitrogen and/or potassium from overfertilising;
> acidic soil; or
> calcium deficiency.

Organic solution

Careful veggie patch practices will reduce the risk of blossom end rot striking, so ensure that you water your garden regularly and adapt to the changing weather conditions — for example, if it has been extremely wet, you won't need to water for a while. Likewise, protect your crops from hot, windy weather so the plants don't dry out. Shadecloth and/or windbreaks will help here, as will mulching your garden beds. Build up your soil with adequate nutrition and prepare it so it drains properly.

If you notice blossom end rot happening year after year, your soil may be calcium-deficient and will require testing. If it is lacking calcium, add lime or gypsum. Calcium deficiency is a symptom of irregular watering, so first follow good watering practices.

Most plants require extra watering when they start to fruit, so be aware of this and water more often to suit. Reapply mulch at this stage too.

Once a fruit has been affected by the condition, there is little you can do to rehabilitate it. The rot, however, can be cut out and the rest of the fruit salvaged for eating.

Leaf blight

Leaf blight is a fungal infection that causes the discolouration and death of plant leaves, and may ultimately result in the death of whole plants. Look for discoloured, yellow or dead leaves on plants. It infects early in the growing season, but the symptoms are most noticeable around harvest time. Leaf blight affects fruiting by limiting the plant's ability to photosynthesise as fruit develops.

Leaf blight is commonly hosted by tomato, potato and strawberry plants, but it can also potentially affect a wider range of veggies, including eggplant, capsicum and cucumber. The disease is a result of damp or humid conditions in the veggie garden, and can be exacerbated by overcrowding, which reduces airflow.

Organic solution

To prevent leaf blight, avoid overcrowding or overwatering your veggie patch. Use drip irrigation instead of fan sprays, and water in the morning, not late in the evening. Buy seeds from reputable seed suppliers, as seeds may carry the disease. Practise crop rotation, as leaf blight may be contained in the soil, and as each case of blight is common to a species, rotating your crops will help avoid reoccurrences.

If you notice leaf blight, pick off the infected leaves and dispose of them properly. If a plant appears terminally ill, dispose of the entire plant. Baking soda sprays like the one used to treat powdery mildew will also have some effect on leaf blight, as will the milk spray remedy (see page 217). Also try making a compost or worm tea by mixing a few handfuls of compost or worm poo in a 10-litre bucket of water, allowing it to settle for some days. Water the affected plants with your tea.

Leaf roll

Leaf roll is a condition whereby, as the name implies, the leaf curls up or rolls. It can occur as the result of inconsistent moisture, exposure to pesticides or viral infection.

The most common type of leaf roll is caused by infrequent or erratic watering practices, which results in the leaf curling up in an effort to promote stronger root growth. Leaf roll is sometimes noticeable after extreme changes in weather conditions — either from wet to dry, or dry to wet. It can also result from severe pruning. Although unsightly, this type of leaf roll is only temporary and not fatal. It can be prevented and

repaired through re-establishing good watering practices and ensuring your soil drains properly.

Leaf roll caused by exposure to pesticides is most common in households where pesticides are used to kill weeds. In addition to leaf rolling, plants will develop twisted growth habits and produce misshapen fruit. The use of pesticides in any shape or form is not recommended, and is considered a last resort; organic remedies and practices should be explored first. If you notice this form of leaf roll but don't use pesticides, investigate whether your neighbour is engaging in the practice. If so, you may need to coax them towards using organic remedies.

The last type of leaf roll, a viral form, is passed on to the plant via sucking insects, such as whiteflies and aphids. It is most common in greenhouses, and rarely occurs in the open veggie patch. The symptoms of viral leaf roll that are not prevalent in the previous two forms include leaves turning purplish or becoming spotted, as well as the leaf texture turning lumpy. Viral leaf roll is the most serious form of the disease. If plants develop viral leaf roll at a young age, it is worthwhile removing these plants, as they are set to suffer a substantial reduction in yield, and it is best to lessen the risk of spreading the disease. Older plants that develop viral leaf roll are at less risk of reduced yield. Pick off leaves as you notice the infection and attempt to maintain control over the whitefly and aphid populations.

Magnesium deficiency

Magnesium deficiency is evident when chlorosis occurs — that is, plant leaves become paler than usual, turning yellow or brown and sometimes dropping off. This symptom will occur on older, lower plant growth first, then spread to the newer growth. In terms of fruiting, magnesium deficiency causes stunted yields, producing smaller and woodier fruit.

This deficiency is the result of very wet conditions, acidic soil or colder than preferable soil conditions. High levels of potassium and calcium, compared with magnesium, will also lead to magnesium deficiency. It is most prevalent on tomato and potato plants that require high levels of potassium to produce fruit, making magnesium unavailable.

Organic solution

To prevent magnesium deficiency, water consistently and test the soil regularly. Mulching will help maintain the soil temperature.

If diagnosed early, magnesium deficiency is easy to treat. Apply a solution of Epsom salts and water directly to the affected leaves and also the roots of the plant (see the instructions on the pack). Your crops will absorb the magnesium through the salts and start to recover.

Powdery mildew

Powdery mildew can be identified by the powdery blotches that form on leaf, stem and sometimes fruit growth. A common plant disease that can affect all plant types, it is caused by humid conditions where there is poor airflow.

As the disease spreads, the spots become larger and spread all over the plant. Although not fatal to a crop, powdery mildew can reduce the plant's ability to photosynthesise and therefore produce fruit.

Organic solution

In the veggie patch, powdery mildew is most prevalent among overcrowded crops that are receiving too much water. Careful water management and crop spacing will help prevent this disease. Try to plant species that are resistant to the disease, and avoid planting non-resistant plants in shady, humid areas. Drip irrigation is best for watering the plants, as wet leaf growth heightens the risk of infection. Get into the habit of watering in the morning — this will allow the patch to dry out during the course of the day.

If you notice the disease on your plants, cut off the affected areas, or consider culling some crops to improve airflow. In the case of fruit trees, thin out the growth by pruning to increase air circulation. You shouldn't fertilise until the problem is contained, as it tends to affect mostly new growth.

A milk spray will also help prevent the disease by protecting the surface of leaves from disease spores. To make such a spray, mix full cream milk in water at a ratio of 1:10.

ACKNOWLEDGEMENTS

Special thanks from us both to:

Mary Small and Ellie Smith, and all at Pan Macmillan, for their professionalism, style, humour and uncanny ability to nearly always find the right music for the moment. Thanks especially for the opportunity to talk about vegetables and everything we love about them, and for helping us make the book we have always wanted to make. It is so satisfying to finally have an audience greater than just the few at our local café, who are forced to listen to our weekly fixture of 'Tomato vs Bean – World's Greatest Vegetable?'

John Laurie and Chris Middleton, for surprising us again and again by making the mundane look beautiful, and for having the surliness to move things along when required.

Michelle Mackintosh, for designing a book that is edible in every sense.

Pauline Haas, our nocturnal typesetter, who worked through so many nights on the book.

Sarah Baker, for an incredible editing job and for teaching us a great deal along the way.

Katrina Varis and family, Ash Gordon and family, Amelia James, Ash Cranston from Little Creatures, Robert Taylor from the Veg Out Community Gardens, Frank Aloi, John Challis, and the Heslop family: Shane, Elise, Charlie and Sam.

Thank you also to Jon Stones and Tico, for coming along for the ride, and taking up the slack in the gardens.

FABIAN

Thank you to my Nonnos and Nonnas, for giving us the opportunity to live in this beautiful country. To my parents: someday I hope to give back all you have given. I love you. Thanks to Mat, to my sister Cathy, and to the rest of my family and friends. And most importantly, thank you to Beck, Jack and Olive.

MAT

First and foremost, thank you to my sister Elise, for the 'set-up' with Fabian. I think our North vs South, Tomato vs Bean, half Italian vs full Italian traits make us a great match. Thank you to Charlie and Sam, too: you are both cheeky and beautiful. Also to Laura 'The Drums' Morgan, Lindsay Williams and Marie Chappatte, for their roles in making this book happen.

Particular thanks must go to FC Barcelona, the Drums, the Antlers, Wild Nothing, Destroyer, Twin Shadow and Jeff Tweedy for getting us through.

Most importantly, I'd like to wholeheartedly thank my Mum and Dad, and Nonna and Nonno (as briefly as I knew him), who have given me everything I need, and more than I could have wanted.

INDEX

A

acidic soil 9, 13
airflow between plants 5, 204
alkaline soil 9, 13
aluminium sulphate 11, 13
Amaryllidaceae (Onion) family 115, 125, 143, 176
annuals, sowing 32
ants 205, 212
apartment no-dig gardens 19
aphids 201, 205, 217
Apiaceae (Carrot) family 95, 100, 113, 152
apple crates
    in informal gardens 5
    as no-dig gardens 20, 21–3
    as raised beds 14
apples 65–6, 208
artichokes, globe 67–9
    Stuffed artichokes 69
asparagus 70–1
    white asparagus 70
Asteraceae (Daisy) family 67, 131
Bacillus thuringiensis (BT) 207–8
balcony vegetable patch 4
basil 117, 119, 213

B

beans
    broad 10, 31, 32, 33, 82–4
    green 72–3
    growing from seed 31, 32
    kids growing 80–1
    trellises for 6, 73
beetroot 31, 33, 74–5
biodiversity 7
birds
    attracting 6
    as pests 207
    as pest controllers 6, 207
black water 24
blanching stems
    celery 101
    leeks 126
blood and bone 10
blossom end rot 215
bok choi 76–7
Brassicaceae (Mustard) family 76, 85, 87, 89, 97, 164, 170, 183, 195, 204, 207

brick edgings 5
broad beans 82–4
    as green manure 10, 83
    growing from seed 31, 32, 33
    as weed suppressants 10
broadcasting (seed sowing) 32
broccoli 33, 85–6, 207
brown (dry) waste 44
brussels sprouts 87–8, 207
BT (Bacillus thuringiensis) 207–8

C

cabbage 33, 89–91, 207
    Cabbage rolls 91
cabbage whiteflies 214
calcium 11
calcium deficiency 215
capital city climatic zones 1
capsicum 33, 92–4, 208, 215
carrots 31, 95–6, 173, 212
caterpillars 201, 207–8
cauliflower 33, 97–9, 207
celery 100–1
chemical sprays 202
Chenopodiaceae (Beet) family 74, 172, 174
chillies 106–8
    Chilli oil 108
chilling hours 55, 66
chives 119
chook manure
    fresh 9, 13
    pellets 10
citrus trees see lemons; limes; oranges
citrus weeing 129
clay soil 8
    fruit trees in 55
    pH balance 9
    water-holding capacity 25
climatic zones
    of capital cities 1
    cool 1
    subtropical 1
    temperate 1
    tropical 1
compacted soil 8, 14
companion planting 6–7
compost
    bays for 44
    brown (dry) waste 44

green (wet) waste 44
    how to use 10
    how it works 43–4
    ideal mix 44
    'juice' from 45
    kitchen waste 44
    'lasagne' of 44
    location for 7
    managing 210
    microbes 43, 44
    non-compostable material 44
    ready to spread 45
    for seed trays 33
    smelly 43, 44, 46
    spreading 45
    temperature inside 44
    trace elements in 9
    trench composting 44
    turning 44
    weeds in 44
compost aerator
    making 47–8
    materials 47
compost bins
    Bokashi unit 44, 45
    rotating wheels 45
    standalone 45
containers and pots see pots and containers
cool climatic zone 1
coriander 119, 205
cottage gardens 5
courtyard 4
cow manure 10
creeping plants 6
crop rotation 6–7, 203–4, 215
cross-pollination 38, 39
cucumber fruit fly 208
cucumbers 6, 109–10, 215
Cucurbitaceae (Gourd) family 109, 161, 179, 197, 208
cypress pine for raised beds 15

D

depth of planting 33
design considerations
    aesthetics 5–6
    air circulation 5, 204
    on balcony 4
    choosing plants 7

companion planting 6–7
  in courtyard 4
  espaliering 6
  frost damage 5
  location 4–5
  pollinators 6
  predators 6
  shade 5
  size 5
  sloping site 5
  sunlight 4–5, 14, 15
  trellising 6, 73
  water sources 6
  for worm farms 7
  see also pots and containers;
  raised beds
detergents in grey water 24
dill 119, 205
diseases
  blossom end rot 215
  indiscriminate spraying 202
  leaf blight 215
  leaf roll 215, 217
  magnesium deficiency 9, 200, 217
  powdery mildew 200, 217
  and wet leaves 6, 25
dolomite lime 11
drainage 5, 6, 14, 15
drilling (seed sowing) 32, 33
drip irrigation
  benefits 6, 25
  mechanism 25
  regulating 25
  seeds and seedlings 25
  and soil composition 25
  supplementing 27
  timer 25, 27
drip irrigation, installing 25
  dimensions 29
  feeder from existing line 27, 28–30
  materials 27
  method 28–31
  where no existing line 31

E
earwigs 208
eco timber (ACQ) for raised beds 15
eelworm 212
eggplant 39, 111–12, 215
espaliering 6, 55, 130, 147

F
Fabaceae (Legume) family 72, 83, 156
fennel 113–14, 205

fertiliser ingredients 9
fish emulsion 11
frost damage 5
fruit flies 201, 208–9
fruit trees
  attracting pollinators and predators 6
  chilling hours 55, 66
  in clay soil 55
  climate for 55
  espaliered 6, 55, 130, 147
  fallen fruit 203
  grafted 55
  irrigating 55
  plant selection 55
  planting 54, 55, 56–8
  pollination 6, 55
  in pots 55
  pruning 59, 66
  for shade 5, 6
  soil preparation 55
  suckers 59
  see also specific fruits
fungal diseases 6, 25

G
gall wasps 130, 201, 209
garden beds, raised see raised
  garden beds
garden hygiene 203
garden lime 11, 13
garlic 115–16, 205
grafted fruit trees 55
green (wet) wastes 44
green manure 10, 83, 204, 212
greenhouse whiteflies 214
grey water
  detergents in 24
  sources 6, 24
gypsum 25, 215

H
hand-pollination 38
hanging baskets 194
heirloom vegetables 37–8
herbs 117–19
  attracting pollinators 6
  in pots 5
  seed-saving 39
honeydew 205, 212, 214
horse manure 10

I
informal gardens 5
insects

as pollinators 6
  see also pests
integrated pest management 202
iron 9

J
jarrah for raised beds 15

K
kaffir lime 135
kids
  educating about food 79, 80
  garden themes for 103–5
  growing beans 80–1
  growing potatoes 159, 167
  growing radishes 164
  mushroom hunting 137
  painting garden tools 121–3
  pulling carrots 95
  scarecrow building 149–51
  seed propagation 31
  water pistol games 189–91
kitchen waste for compost 44

L
ladybirds 205, 209, 212
leaf blight 215
leaf miners 209
leaf roll 215, 217
leafy greens
  in pots 5
  seed-harvesting 39
  sunlight needs 4
leeks 125–6
legumes
  as green manure 10
  weed suppressants 10
lemons 6, 129, 130, 147, 209
lettuce 33, 131–3, 212
Liliaceae (Lily) family 70
limes 6, 25, 130, 134–6, 147
location of vegetable garden 4–5
lucerne hay mulch 26

M
magnesium 11
magnesium deficiency 9, 200, 217
mains water 6, 24
manure
  chook 9, 10, 13
  cow 10
  green 10, 83, 204, 212
  horse 10
  to improve water retention 25

nitrogen in 9–10
  trace elements in 9
marigolds 205, 212
Mediterranean fruit fly 208
merbau for raised beds 15
mint 119
mirrors in small gardens 5
mulch
  applying 26
  composition 26
  improving water retention 26
  for seedlings 26
  trace elements in 9
  weed suppressant 26, 203
mushrooms 137–9
mustard greens 205

N
nasturtiums 205, 213
netting for pests 207, 210
newspaper pots 33
nitrogen
  in compost 10
  in manures 9–10
  in soil 9
nitrogen fixers 83
nitrogen-greedy plants 83
no-dig garden
  for apartments 19
  benefits 19
  maintenance 19
  organic matter 19
  settling 23
  within raised garden bed 19
no-dig garden, building
  depth 20
  materials 19–20, 21
  over lawn or existing bed 20
  with recycled apple crates 20, 21–3
Nonna's recipes
  Cabbage rolls 91
  Chilli oil 108
  Marinated olives 142
  Stuffed artichokes 69
  Sugo 194
  Zucchini flower broken eggs 199
nutrients for plants 200, 211
  nitrogen 9–10
  phosphorus 1, 9, 11
  potassium 1, 9, 10, 11
nutrients for soil (organic)
  aluminium sulphate 11, 13
  blood and bone 10
  chook manure (fresh) 9, 13

chook manure (pellets) 10
cow manure 10
dolomite lime 11
fish emulsion 11
garden lime 11, 13
green manure 10, 83, 204, 212
horse manure 10
seaweed extract 11
wood ash 11, 13
worm castings 10, 49, 53
see also compost

O
Oleaceae (Olive) family 141
olives 141–2
  Marinated olives 142
olive oil 141, 142
onions 7, 143–4
open pollination 37, 38
oranges 6, 145–7
oregano 119
organic gardening
  hygiene 203–4
  pest control 202
  restoring pH levels 9–11
  water retention 25
  see also nutrients for soil
overcrowded plants 204, 215

P
pak choi 76–7
parasitic wasps 209, 212
parsley 119
parsnips 152–3, 212
Passifloraceae (Passionfruit) family 154
passionfruit 154–5
pea straw mulch 26
peas 156–7
  as green manure 10
  growing from seed 31, 32, 34–6
  trellises for 6
  as weed suppressants 10
perlite 8
pest control
  indiscriminate spraying 202
  integrated pest management 202
  netting 207, 210
  organic approach 202
  pets as deterrents 207, 210, 212
  and pruning 59
  reduced with drip-hose watering 25
pesticides 217
pests
  ants 205, 212

aphids 201, 205, 217
birds 207
caterpillars 201, 207–8
cucumber fruit fly 208
earwigs 208
eelworm 212
fruit flies 201, 208–9
gall wasps 130, 201, 209
leaf miners 209
Mediterranean fruit fly 208
possums 200, 209–10
Queensland fruit fly 208
rodents 200, 210, 212
root-knot nematodes 212
scale 212
slugs and snails 145, 200, 205, 213
thrips 213–14
white cabbage butterfly 207
white cabbage moth 85, 86, 91, 207
whiteflies 214
pets as pest deterrents 207, 210, 212
pH levels
  and climate 9
  natural balance in soil 9
  restoring 9–11
  testing 12–13
phosphorus 1, 9, 11
plant diversity 204
plant nutrition 9
planting
  companion planting 6–7
  depth for seeds 33
  fruit trees 54, 55, 56–8
  overcrowded plants 204, 215
Poaceae (Maize) family 185
pollination
  attracting pollinators 6
  cross-pollination 38, 39
  fruit trees 6, 55
  hand-pollination 38
  open pollination 37, 38
  self-pollination 38, 55
possums 200, 209–10
potash 10
potassium 1, 9, 10, 11
potatoes 158–60, 212, 215
  spud towers 160, 166–9
pots and containers
  fruit trees 55
  herbs 5
  leafy greens 5
  lime trees 130, 135
  lemon trees 129
  matching pots 5

newspaper pots 33
as raised beds 14
seed-raising mixes 32
soil 8
sowing in 33
tomatoes 194
potting mixes 9
powdery mildew 200, 217
predators 6
pruning fruit trees 59, 66
pumpkin 161–3, 208

Q

Queensland fruit fly 208

R

radishes 31, 164–5
railway sleepers for raised beds 15
rainfall
    and pH levels 9
    seasonal 24
rainwater tanks
    benefits 6
    collection potential 24
    location 4, 6
raised beds
    benefits 5–6, 14
    drainage 6
    incorporating no-dig garden 19
    pots and containers 14
    recycled wooden crates as 14
    settling the soil 14, 18
    using recycled print cartridges 15
raised beds, building
    access considerations 14
    height 15
    materials 15, 16
    step-by-step 17–18
    tools 16
    width and length 14–15
recipes see Nonna's recipes
recycled materials
    apple crates 5, 14, 20, 21–3
    golf-club trellis 104–5
    for informal look 5
    for no-dig garden 20
    print cartridges 15
    as raised beds 14, 15
    themes for kids 103
    timbers 15
red gum for raised beds
    new timber 15
    recycled timber 15
rocket 170–1

rodents 200, 210, 212
root vegetables 4
root-knot nematodes 212
Rosaceae (Rose) family 65, 181
rosemary 117, 119
rotten (fallen) fruit 203
Rutaceae (Citrus) family 129, 135, 145

S

sandy loam 8
sandy soil 8
    fruit trees in 55
    pH balance 9
    water-holding capacity 25
scale 212
scarecrow-building 149–51, 205
seaweed extract 11
seed propagation
    benefits 31
    for kids 31
    sourcing seeds 31, 37–8
    see also seed sowing
seed saving 31
    benefits 37, 38
    drying 39
    fruiting plants 39
    harvesting 39
    herbs 39
    heirloom seeds 37–8
    non-fruiting plants 39
    pests or diseases 39
    planting 39
    preparing 39
    record-keeping 38
    selection factors 38
    from self-pollinators 38
    storing 39
    tomatoes 38, 39, 40–3
seed sowing
    advantage over seedlings 31
    annuals 32
    broadcasting 32
    composting 32
    depth of planting 32, 33
    drilling 32, 33
    peas 31, 32, 34–6
    in pots 33
    in rows 32
    in seed trays 33
    seed-raising mixes 32
    in situ 32–3
    soaking seeds 32
    soil preparation 32
    soil temperature 32

spacing 33
thinning 33
watering 25, 27
seed trays
    with cells 33, 34–6
    compost 33
    soil 33
    thinning 33
    watering 33
seedlings
    acclimatising 31, 33
    mulching 26
    watering 25, 27
seed-raising mixes 32
seeds
    hybrids 37–8
    old and heirloom varieties 37–8
    sourcing 31, 37–8
    see also seed sowing
self-pollinating plants
    citrus trees 55
    seed saving 38
shade barriers 5
shadecloths 215
silt soil 8
silverbeet 172–3, 212
silverleaf whiteflies 214
size of vegetable garden 5
sloping site 5
slugs and snails 145, 200, 205, 213
small gardens
    apartment 19
    balcony 4
    courtyard 4
    mirrors in 5
    vegetables for 7
    see also pots and containers
soil
    air pockets 8
    buying 8
    compacted 8, 14
    composition and watering 25
    feeding 8
    for seed propagation 32
    friable 8
    health 203
    ideal 8
    microbes in 43–4
    particle size 8
    pH levels 9
    and plant nutrition 9–11
    preparing 55
    settling 14, 18
    temperature 1

testing pH level 12–13
tilling 19, 32
waterlogged 8
see also nutrients for soil (organic)
soil types
   acidic 9, 13
   alkalaine 9, 13
   clay 8, 9, 25, 55
Solanaceae (Nightshade) family 93, 107, 111, 159, 193, 204
sooty mould 205, 212, 214
sowing see seed sowing
spinach 174–5
spraying for diseases 202
spring onions 176–7
spud towers 160, 166–9
squash 178–80
stem rot 26
stinging nettles 213
strawberries 7, 181–2, 215
subtropical climatic zone 1
sunlight hours 4–5, 14, 15
swede 183–4
sweetcorn 7, 94, 185–7

T
Tassie oak for raised beds 15
temperate climatic zone 1
The Little Veggie Patch Co 15, 159, 193
   formation ix
   philosophy ix–x
thinning seedlings 33
thrips 213–14
thyme 117, 119
tilling 19, 32
tomato grubs 200
tomatoes 33, 192–4, 208, 212, 215
   planting after broad beans 7
   in pots 194
   seed saving 38, 39, 40–3
   Sugo 194
   trellises for 6
tools
   kids painting 121–3
   misplacing 121
trace elements 9, 200, 217
transplantation stress 31
trellising 6, 73
   golf-club trellis 104–5
trench composting 44
trenching 125
tropical climatic zone 1
turnips 195–6

V
vegetables
   acidic soil for 9
   fruiting 39
   heirloom 37–8
   'windy' 89, 113
vermicomposting 49–53

W
waste
   brown (dry) 44
   green (wet) 44
water
   diseases and wet foliage 25, 203
   games with (insect control) 189–91
   importance 24
water retention improvement
   with compost 25
   with lime or gypsum 25
   with manure 25
   with mulch 26
water sources
   black water 24
   grey water 6, 24
   mains water 6, 24
   rainwater tanks 6, 24
watering
   drip system 6, 25, 27, 203
   sprays 25
waterlogged soil 8
wee
   citrus wee 129
   worm wee 49, 50, 51, 52
weeds 203
   activated by tilling 19
   in compost 44
   hosting root-knot nematodes 212
   suppressing 10, 26, 203
wet leaves and plant diseases 6, 25
white cabbage butterfly 207
white cabbage moth 85, 86, 91, 207
whiteflies 217
   cabbage 214
   greenhouse 214
   silverleaf 214
windbreaks 215
wood ash 11, 13
worm farm
   benefits 7, 49
   food likes and dislikes 50
   food preparation 50
   when to feed 50
   worm breeds 49
   worm reproduction 50

worm farm construction 52–3
   levels 50
   location 7, 49
   materials for 51
worm poo (castings) 49, 53
   how to use 10
worm wee 49, 50, 51, 52

Z
zinc 9
zucchini 39, 197–9, 208
   Zucchini flower broken eggs 199